CHRIST
MY GOOD
SHEPHERD

A Bible Study on Psalm 23

Daniel T. Rogers

ISBN: 978-1-917667-62-3 (sc)

ISBN: 978-1-917667-61-6 (hc)

Print information available on the last page.

To my grandchildren,

May you see the beauty, love, and care of the Good Shepherd even in the hard times. Because he is with you, you can be bold as lions.

Acknowledgments

I would like to thank my Good Shepherd, who has cared for and sustained me all these years. I trust you to carry me home.

And, to my wife, Jane, for her support and love over these last 30+ years that allowed me to put this work together.

Finally, thanks to my brother, Paul, for his tireless work—reading, editing, and encouraging. Your church is blessed to have you.

Contents

Chapter 1

I Am His and He Is Mine

"The Lord is my shepherd; I shall not want..." Psalm 23:1

If you survey people as to the most well-known passages in the Bible, you would probably get answers like John 3:16 for evangelism, 1 Corinthians 13 for weddings, or the Lord's Prayer when facing death. The problem with well-known passages is that we know them so well we tend to either read them without thinking about them or listen without really listening.

I would argue that this is true even for Psalm 23. If we had never heard the Psalm before but knew the gospel in all its splendor, we would look at this short passage and marvel. We would marvel because it touches on most themes dealing with salvation, adoption, justification, sanctification, life, death, resurrection, and eternity. All in six little verses.

We don't know whether David wrote this Psalm early in his life or towards the end. Either way, it truly does give insight into a heart that seeks after God. It gives us a picture of why God would say that David was a man after his own heart (Acts 13:22). There is within this Psalm a true picture of the Sabbath rest we have in Christ—both now and in the life to come. I use the word rest very deliberately. It denotes a fellowship with him that engages all the senses, all of our effort, and all of our affections. We have found redemption in our relationships, our work, and our play. This rest is seen vividly in Psalm 46 with the famous climax: "Be still, and know that I am God."

Psalm 23 is written to give Christians encouragement in this life, no matter the place, time, or circumstance. Why we wait to read it at funerals, I will never know. The encouragement it gives for life is beyond measure. Over the next few chapters, follow along with me, bask in his grace, and be encouraged by his promises. With that said, here at the start, let's consider what I would call the "what" and the "so what."

The "what" covers what I consider to be the clear declarations within the passage. At the very least, we see these:

(1) A declaration we are his and he is ours

(2) A declaration of providence

(3) A declaration of provision

(4) A declaration of protection

(5) A declaration of deliverance

I am sure there are more. We could argue semantics and say others are either included or not in this list, but we will suffice these for now. The point I want us to grasp is that the "what" points to the "so what."

The "so what" answers the question: "If these declarations are true, then what does it mean for life? What are the implications?" I would argue that if we come face to face with the "what," the "so what" will open our eyes and hearts to real hope and encouragement in a world that can be dark and lost. The "so what" includes things like the following that we read about in this Psalm:

(1) Hope

(2) Rest

(3) Contentment

(4) Confidence

(5) Joy

(6) Life

(7) Forgiveness

(8) Goodness

This is what the "what" gives us as part of the gospel and our inheritance in him.

Psalm 23 points clearly to the coming messiah and the work he would do. This picture of the messiah as a Good Shepherd can be seen across the pages of scripture. Read Ezekiel 34:11–24. Notice the motif of the shepherd caring for the flock, leading them where they needed to go, and teaching them obedience. As you do, pick up on some of the "what" statements that we see in Psalm 23. For example:

(1) A declaration we are his and he is ours

    a. "I myself will search for my sheep and will seek them out"

    b. "As a shepherd seeks out his flock when he is among his sheep that have been scattered, so will I seek out my sheep"

    c. "I myself will be the shepherd of my sheep"

(2) A declaration of providence

    a. "The fat and the strong I will destroy. I will feed them in justice"

    b. "And I will judge between sheep and sheep"

(3) A declaration of provision

    a. "And I will feed them on the mountains of Israel, by the ravines, and in all the inhabited places of the country"

    b. "There they shall lie down in good grazing land, and on rich pasture they shall feed"

    c. "I myself will make them lie down"

(4) A declaration of protection

    a. "I will bind up the injured, and I will strengthen the weak, and the fat and the strong I will destroy"

(5) A declaration of deliverance

    a. "I will rescue them from all places where they have been scattered"

    b. "I will seek the lost, and I will bring back the strayed."

This is the picture of Christ in the Gospels. Christ is the Good Shepherd. At the start of his ministry, Jesus stood up in the synagogue (Luke 4:16) and quoted Isaiah 61:1-2 which says: "The Spirit of the Lord GOD is upon me, because the LORD has anointed me to bring good news to the poor; he has sent me to bind up the brokenhearted, to proclaim liberty to the captives, and the opening of the prison to those who are bound; to proclaim the year of the LORD's favor." He sat down and, as everyone was looking at him, he said, "Today this Scripture has been fulfilled in your hearing." Jesus was saying, "I am the Good Shepherd who has come. All of what this verse talks about – good news and the Lord's favor, that is fulfilled in me and can be found nowhere else."

Getting back to the Ezekiel 34 passage, we see this even more clearly. Hear what God says next to the sheep of his pasture: "I will make with them a covenant of peace... And I will make them and the places all around my hill a blessing, and I will send down the showers in their season; they shall be showers of blessing." Christ is the Good Shepherd.

We hear this echoed again in Jeremiah 23:1-6: "Then I will gather the remnant of my flock out of all the countries where I have driven them, and I will bring them back to their fold, and they shall be fruitful and multiply. I will set shepherds over them who will care for them, and they shall fear no more, nor be dismayed, neither shall any be missing, declares the LORD. Behold, the days are coming, declares the LORD, when I will raise up for David a righteous Branch, and he shall reign as king and deal wisely, and shall execute justice and righteousness in the land. In his days Judah will be saved, and Israel will dwell securely. And this is the name by which he will be called: 'The LORD is our righteousness.'"

Do you see it now? All of the Old Testament points to the Good Shepherd who would come and be the "what" so that we could live "so what" kind of lives. Jesus is the fulfillment of all the Old Testament points. There is no other. There is no other way to salvation except through Christ. Don't miss his "what."

Yes, Psalm 23 is about our Savior and Lord who came to seek and save that which was lost. He saw those who were following him (Mark 6) as sheep without a shepherd. And so, he began to tend to them. He began to teach them (rod and staff). This was, after all, his ministry throughout. To tend, to gather, to care, to heal, to save. This is what Isaiah declared in Is 40:11. "He will tend his flock like a shepherd; he will gather the lambs in his arms; he will carry them in his bosom, and gently lead those that are with young."

Jesus was clear in his claim to be the Good Shepherd. Let's consider John 10:1–18. Jesus says these words in response to the religious leaders of his day: "**I am the good shepherd.** The good shepherd lays down his life for the sheep. He who is a hired hand and not a shepherd, who does not own the sheep, sees the wolf coming and leaves the sheep and flees, and the wolf snatches them and scatters them. He flees because he is a hired hand and cares nothing for the sheep. **I am the good shepherd.** I know my own and my own know me, just as the Father knows me and I know the Father; and I lay down my life for the sheep. And I have other sheep that are not of this fold. I must bring them also, and they will listen to my voice. So there will be one flock, one shepherd."

Walking through this passage, what are the characteristics of the Good Shepherd from the passages above? The Good Shepherd knows his sheep, he protects his sheep, he provides for his sheep, he rescues his sheep. Don't miss the significance of what Jesus is saying here.

First, he says that the Good Shepherd "lays down his life for the sheep." The hired hand, when danger arises, will never give his life for something that is not his. The hired hand sees the wolf, sees the danger, and runs, leaving the sheep to be killed and scattered. The Good Shepherd, though, lays down his life for the sheep. He stands in the gap. He takes what is ours and gives what is his and, in so doing, saves his people and reconciles them to God. Jesus does this willingly and freely. What happened during Easter week was not a picture of someone's life being taken but rather of a life being given.

Second, he says that he calls his sheep and they listen to his voice. "I know my own and my own know me." This is a declaration of ownership—we are his and he is ours! He calls to us and we listen. He calls to us and we believe. He calls to us and we follow (Matthew 4:19-20; 4:21-22; 9:9). A sheep knows the voice of the shepherd. This is the test of whether you are his sheep or not. Do you know his voice? Do you know his word? Do you cherish his voice? Do you follow his voice?

Third, he calls to himself sheep not just from Israel but from all nations. "And I have other sheep that are not of this fold. I must bring them also, and they will listen to my voice." We have hope in these words. We are not lost. He will seek us out just as he did those in Israel. Here is the cool part.

Fourth, in him, is the unity of all the sheep. "So there will be one flock, one shepherd." We are called to unity—the unity of the Spirit. John Piper talks about this unity in the following manner: "This text shows that, in a decisive act of atonement and reconciliation, Christ has already made us one. What he has accomplished at Calvary we should maintain by the Spirit. But in another sense the unity Christ purchased and guaranteed with his blood must now be lived out and brought to full expression in the life of the church. In this sense it is a goal to be attained."[1]

To sum up the "what," the Good Shepherd is the Lord. He is mine and I am his. What I see in this statement, "The Lord is my shepherd," is that he is my redeemer; he is my providence, my provision, and my protection. The Lord is my shepherd. He lays down his life for me. He calls me. He seeks me out. He brings unity to his people, the sheep of his pasture. I pray this day that we will listen for his voice, know his voice, and follow after him seeking the comfort of his fold.

If the statement "the Lord is my Shepherd" is true, then what does that mean for my life? This gets us to the "so what" that we mentioned at the start. For anyone who views Christ as their shepherd, the next statement naturally follows: "I shall not want." These words from Psalm 23:1 are a statement of an individual who has been through much and, looking back, sees the providential hand of the Almighty guiding, correcting, rebuking, mending, loving, and leading in every step and detail.

What does "I shall not want" imply? To be clear, the phrase "I shall not want" doesn't mean that we get everything we desire. Rather, it means that we have everything that we need. It is the same word that we see in Exodus 16:18 when, during the wilderness years, the people of Israel "had no lack." We see it again in Deuteronomy 2:7 when Moses says, "These forty years the Lord your God has been with you. You have *lacked nothing.*" This was the same promise God made concerning the promised land in Deuteronomy 8:9: "a land in which... *you will lack nothing.*"

David, as he wrote the words "I shall not want," views the Good Shepherd for who he is and what he has done, and declares with confidence that he will lack nothing. After all, if the shepherd can care for the whole of Israel, he could provide for one person. This is the confidence of a believer as his faith is bolstered by the character of God.

The action words in Psalm 23 truly demonstrate how the Good Shepherd cares for the sheep and why the psalmist can say with confidence that he needs nothing. We see it in the making, the leading, and the restoring. We see it in the preparing, the anointing, and the dwelling. David, looking back on his life—how Saul chased after him to kill him and how his own son sought to dethrone him, could see clearly his shepherd caring for him.

Do the gospels give us this same picture of Jesus? Mark 6:30-43 is an example of Jesus fulfilling his role as Good Shepherd. In that passage, he feeds the 5000. Hear the story recounted by Mark. "The apostles returned to Jesus and told him all that they had done and taught. And he said to them, 'Come away by yourselves to a desolate place and rest a while.' For many were coming and going, and they had no leisure even to eat. And they went away in the boat to a desolate place by themselves. Now many saw them going and recognized them, and they ran there on foot from all the towns and got there ahead of them. When he went ashore, he saw a great crowd, and he had compassion on them, because they were like sheep without a shepherd. And he began to teach them many things. And when it grew late, his disciples came to him and said, 'This is a desolate place, and the hour is now late. Send them away to go into the surrounding countryside and villages and buy themselves something to eat.' But he answered them, 'You give them something to eat.' And they said to him, 'Shall we go and buy two hundred denarii worth of bread and give it to them to eat?' And he said to them, 'How many loaves do you have? Go and see.' And when they had found out, they said, 'Five, and two fish.' Then he commanded them all to sit down in groups on the green grass. So they sat down in groups, by hundreds and by fifties. And taking the five loaves and the two fish, he looked up to heaven and said a blessing and broke the loaves and gave them to the disciples to set before the people. And he divided the two fish among them all. And they all ate and were satisfied. And they took up twelve baskets full of broken pieces and of the fish. And those who ate the loaves were five thousand men."

Many theologians say that the feeding of the 4000 and the 5000 are fulfillments of Psalm 23. What happened when Jesus saw the crowd, and how did he see them? First, as he saw the crowd, he had compassion on them. He entered into their suffering. Second, as the Good Shepherd, he saw them as sheep without a shepherd and took up that mantle. What they needed, he gave them. Scripture tells us that he healed many and taught them. As sheep without a shepherd, he fed them spiritually and cared for them. Third, he gave them a place to rest in the green grass. Finally, as his disciples came to have him send them away towards the end of the day so that they could all go and find a place to eat, Jesus took care of that need as well, providing for their physical needs.

Matthew Henry says this about the miracle: "This miracle was significant, and shows that Christ came into the world, to be the great feeder as well as the great healer; not only to restore, but to preserve and nourish, spiritual life; and in him there is enough for all that come to him, enough to fill the soul, to fill the treasures; none are sent empty away from Christ, but those that come to him full of themselves."[2]

I agree that this picture of the feeding of the 4000 and 5000 is a fulfillment of this Psalm. It is a proof text for those looking to Christ as the source of all they need. This is why he taught us to pray: "Give us this day our daily bread." "I shall not want" should grant us great encouragement, even in the common grace of provision, that we are his and he is ours. He delights in us as his children and will provide all that we need. It points us to his redemption and mercy.

And so, we have these encouraging words of the provision of our Good Shepherd over and over:

- "Therefore I tell you, do not be anxious about your

life, what you will eat or what you will drink, nor about your body, what you will put on. Is not life more than food, and the body more than clothing? Look at the birds of the air: they neither sow nor reap nor gather into barns, and yet your heavenly Father feeds them. Are you not of more value than they?" Matthew 6:25-26

- "Cast your burden upon the Lord and He will sustain you; He will never allow the righteous to be shaken." Psalm 55:22

- "The young lions do lack and suffer hunger; But they who seek the Lord shall not be in want of any good thing." Psalm 34:10

- "The Lord God made garments of skin for Adam and his wife, and clothed them." Genesis 3:21

- "Come to Me, all who are weary and heavy-laden, and I will give you rest." Matthew 11:28

These demonstrate the "so what" living the Good Shepherd offers his sheep. It represents a life filled with hope, rest, contentment, confidence, joy, life, forgiveness, and goodness. If you know Christ as the Good Shepherd, you can rest in the provision he has for you and know that in all things, you will lack nothing in him. This is the promise of the gospel.

Study Questions

(1) How does this Psalm picture of the Sabbath rest we have in Christ?

(2) How does Ezekiel 34:11–24 provide a picture of Christ and his ministry?

(3) How does Jeremiah 23:1–6 foreshadow John 10:1–18?

(4) In what ways do you see Psalm 23 fulfilled in Mark 6:30–43?

(5) In what ways do you declare "I shall not want?"

(6) In what areas of your life are you not declaring "I shall not want?"

(7) How do the following words encourage you to surrender those areas where you are not saying: "I shall not want?" Matthew 6:25–26, Psalm 55:22, Psalm 34:10, Genesis 3:21, and Matthew 11:28. What will you do to surrender them?

Chapter 2

His Provision, Providence and Protection

"He makes...He leads...He restores..." Psalm 23:2-3a

In the first verse of Psalm 23, we are taught that we are his and he is ours. We called the statements that flowed from that thesis the "what" and the "so what" of life. They represent more than a preference but are a controlling factor in our lives. Beginning in verse 2, David begins to expound on what "I shall not want" really means. We see three phrases that give us insight—he makes, he leads, and he restores. These three words are key to understanding and living "so what" lives for him. They show us:

(1) His provision for us

(2) His providence over us

(3) His protection of us

First, let's consider his provision for us. Notice the words: green pastures, still waters, restores my soul. He is the source of all we need. In all things, he provides for our physical needs. In all things, he provides for our spiritual needs. In all things, he not only redeems us but seeks after us.

The abundant life that he provides to us is not necessarily one in which we get everything we ask for; receive only health and wealth; or that life will be easy and without trouble. But it is a life that is abundant and abundantly good for us no matter where we find ourselves. Hear what scripture says about this abundant life he offers.

- "I came that they may have life and have it abundantly." John 10:10b

- "I am the bread of life; whoever comes to me shall not hunger, and whoever believes in me shall never thirst." John 6:35

- "Come to me all who labor and are heavy laden, and I will give you rest. Take my yoke upon you, and learn from me, for I am gentle and lowly in heart, and you will find rest for your souls. For my yoke is easy, and my burden is light." Matthew 11:28–30

- "He who did not spare his own Son but gave him up for us all, how will he not also with him graciously give us all things?" Romans 8:32

As we can see from these passages, the provision he provides for our soul leads to a life that is both abundant and fulfilling. Jesus, in his discussion about this abundant life in Mark 9, uses this phrase repeatedly, reminding us of his provision for our souls: "it is better to enter the kingdom of God." It is better. Don't miss that as you look at temptation and see the pleasure it might bring in the near term. Remember, the provision of your soul is better. His provision, his way, his leading is better.

That is why Jesus taught us to pray: "Give us this day, our daily bread." It sets our minds upon his provision in all things that follow. In doing this, we acknowledge the source of our provision, the graciousness of our provision, and the surety of our provision. When saying that he makes us lie down in green pastures, leads us beside still waters, and restores our souls, we declare with the psalmist that our Good Shepherd is the source of all we need. We need to look nowhere else.

How is the Good Shepherd the source of all we need? He leads us to where the meadows filled with green grass are. He knows where the waters of rest are located. He knows what our very souls need. He knows; he leads; we follow. The sheep follow the leading and control of their shepherd.

From this part of the Psalm, we see something really sweet. We cannot help but be pointed to his redemption in the restoration of our souls.

What images or thoughts come to your mind when you read the words "He restores my soul?" We imagine pictures of the many graces he gives each day that point us to the day when the riches immeasurable in him will be seen. No more I will we know the pangs of hunger; no more will we know the pain that comes from our decaying bodies; no more will we know the loneliness and darkness in our souls that wonder if we are loved. In this part of the Psalm, we see a pointing to a mansion he went to prepare for us; we see a people he is gathering to himself; we see a never-ending banquet feast. We see the eternal future he has prepared for us—a future where there are no tears, no pain, no sorrow.

Think about the feeding of the 5000 and 4000 that we discussed last chapter. He sits them on the green grass. He gives them rest. He teaches them the life-giving words of the gospel. He feeds them, meeting their physical needs. But not only that. To restore is to return or to bring back. The ultimate in restoration is getting back to Eden. This he provides in his providence to his sheep.

We see this restoration pictured in the messianic Psalm preceding this one as well. We read: "All the ends of the earth shall remember and turn to the Lord, and all the families of the nations shall worship before you" (Psalm 22:27). This verse comes after these words in Psalm 22:1: "My God, my God, why have you forsaken me?" These were the words Christ our Good Shepherd cried out while hanging on the cross purchasing our restoration. His pursuit of our restoration, the price he paid to redeem us, is seen in these words.

We see this even more beautifully pictured in the parable of the lost sheep. "What man of you, having a hundred sheep, if he has lost one of them, does not leave the ninety-nine in the open country, and go after the one that is lost, until he finds it? And when he has found it, he lays it on his shoulders, rejoicing. And when he comes home, he calls together his friends and his neighbors, saying to them, 'Rejoice with me, for I have found my sheep that was lost.' Just so, I tell you, there will be more joy in heaven over one sinner who repents than over ninety-nine righteous persons who need no repentance." Luke 15:4-7

The fact "he makes, he leads, he restores" should grant us great encouragement that we are his and he is ours; he delights in us as his children, and he will provide all that we need. It points us to his redemption and mercy. I once heard it said: "The good news is that you are not alone – someone is looking for you."

Second, let's consider his providence over our lives, as seen in this passage. Notice the words: he makes me, he leads me, he restores my soul. In all things, he is completing the good work he began in us. In all things, he is driving us to the promised land. In all things, he is reversing the curse, providing new life, new work, new relationships, and a new dwelling. My sheep hear my voice, Jesus says, and they follow me (John 10:27–28). Follow me, Jesus says, and I will make you into fishers of men (Mark 1:16–20).

Notice in these words that the "Shepherd King is sovereignly guiding David to his abundance and giving him a place to dwell."[1] Even amid trial or struggle, there is a trusting in the providence of God over our lives that even those times, when viewed through the lenses of his grace, are turned into meadows of luscious green pastures. As we see that, we will understand that nothing can separate us from him.

There is happiness in his providence as we are placed where he wants us (green pastures), guided where he takes us (waters that are still), and helped as he gives us the grace needed for life (restores). Matthew Henry wrote: "We have the supports and comforts of this life from God's good hand, our daily bread from him as our Father. The greatest abundance is but a dry pasture to a wicked man, who relishes that only in it which pleases the senses; but to the godly man, who tastes the goodness of God in all his enjoyments, and by faith relishes that, though he has but little of the world, it is a green pasture...God makes his saints to lie down; he gives them quiet and contentment in their own minds, whatever their lot is; their souls dwell at ease in him, and that makes every pasture green...Let us not think it enough to pass through them, but let us lie down in them, abide in them; this is my rest forever. It is by a constancy of the means of grace that the soul is fed."[2]

The gospel does change everything. It changes our perspective. We respond in contentment to what is going on around us. We find peace during the storms of life, realizing that life with our Good Shepherd is better. Outside of the gospel, we see a life where "the greatest abundance is but a dry pasture to a wicked man, who relishes that only in it which pleases the senses."

Again, "Those that feed on God's goodness must follow his direction; he leads them by his providence, by his word, by his Spirit, disposes their affairs for the best, according to his counsel, disposes their affections and actions according to his command, directs their eye, their way, and their heart, into his love."[3]

The gospel changes everything. We want to live under the rule and authority of our Good Shepherd, for his yoke is easy and the burden is light (Matt 11:29–30). We begin to pray, "thy will be done," understanding that it is better to be ruled by him in all things and all places. It is better than the hamster wheel this world offers, where there is no rest, no purpose, no relief, and no end. The gospel offers green pastures, still waters, and restoration. Simply believe the good news and follow Christ.

How is the imagery in Psalm 23:2–3b a reflection of the gospel? It is from these still waters that we begin to see the gospel, its refreshing nature, life-giving nature, and resting nature. Jesus, talking with the Samaritan at the well, said: "Jesus answered her, 'If you knew the gift of God, and who it is that is saying to you, 'Give me a drink,' you would have asked him, and he would have given you living water.' The woman said to him, 'Sir, you have nothing to draw water with, and the well is deep. Where do you get that living water? Are you greater than our father Jacob? He gave us the well and drank from it himself, as did his sons and his livestock.' Jesus said to her, 'Everyone who drinks of this water will be thirsty again, but whoever drinks of the water that I will give him will never be thirsty again. The water that I will give him will become in him a spring of water welling up to eternal life'" (John 4).

The place of rest is not a place but a person—God himself. And it is a gift. We must surrender to him to experience the refreshing, life-giving, and resting nature of the waters of the gospel. They are not rapids but cool and still. This is the key: "You would have asked him, and he would have given you living water." Surrender to him is the trusting of faith. It is believing in him as both Savior and Lord.

I remember years ago hearing the illustration that Evangelism Explosion gave concerning faith. They would take a chair and say: "Do you see this chair?" The answer would be yes. They would then ask, "Do you see the chair's construction? Do you think it would hold you up if you sat in it?" The answer would again be yes. Finally, they would say, "Sit in the chair." Trust that the chair will hold you. Give up your control. Sit in the chair. That is what his providence looks like. We submit to him and trust him completely to hold us up. In his providence, he holds us and provides.

Third, his protection of his sheep. Follow what David says. In taking us to these places; in giving us rest; in redeeming our lives, time, work, and everything else, the Good Shepherd has promised that the Father will not let even one of these given to him to perish. He would not take them to a place where he could not keep them. The Father will hold them in his hand and no one is greater than the Father to pry open that hand and steal away one of his (John 10:29).

One of the key doctrines of the reformed faith is the perseverance of the saints or the preservation of the saints. This doctrine reminds us that our salvation is not up to us, secured by us, or determined by us. Rather, God himself has determined it, the Son accomplished it, and the Spirit applies and seals it. This gives me great hope that even though I am prone to wander, the shepherd pursues me and brings me back. Not one of his sheep will he lose. Not one of his sheep can wander off too far that they cannot come back. Not one of his sheep can get lost to where they can never be found again. No, the shepherd pursues those of his that are lost, wandering, and in danger bringing them back to him and his fold.

A picture of this protection and pursuit of lost sheep can be seen in the life of David, who wrote Psalm 23. The story begins in springtime. Armies were heading into war. Typically, the king would go with his army. However, this time, the king (David) decided to stay behind in Jerusalem. Late one afternoon, David arose and went for a walk on the roof of his palace, where he could see much of the city. And, in the distance, he saw a woman, Bathsheba. She was the daughter of a valued advisor and the wife of a valiant soldier, Uriah the Hittite. Not only was Uriah a valiant soldier, he was a faithful soldier, one of David's mighty warriors. As the story goes, David sinned, and soon afterward he received word that Bathsheba was expecting. So, David concocted a plan to get Uriah home to cover his sin. When Uriah didn't fall into

David's plan, David had him killed. He then took Bathsheba as his wife. David thought this was the end of the story.

But God sent Nathan, the prophet, to see David. Nathan tells him a story about two men, one rich and the other poor. In the story, the rich man wantonly takes the only thing of value to the poor man. At this, David is incensed and says: "As the LORD lives, the man who has done this deserves to die, and he shall restore the lamb fourfold, because he did this thing, and because he had no pity."

With the trap set, Nathan declared: "You are the man!" Hear what he says next as it is important: "Thus says the LORD, the God of Israel, 'I anointed you king over Israel, and I delivered you out of the hand of Saul. And I gave you your master's house and your master's wives into your arms and gave you the house of Israel and of Judah. And if this were too little, I would add to you as much more."

Hear David's response: "David said to Nathan, 'I have sinned against the LORD.' And Nathan said to David, 'The LORD also has put away your sin; you shall not die.'"

God, in his protection and pursuit of his people, will not let them lie in the depths of their sin or leave them in the depths of the pig pen. He graciously pursues us and restores us, saves us, heals us, binds us, loves us, and provides for us. This is the incredible story of the gospel found here in this beautiful Psalm. May you know this grace and may you experience his peace as he graciously provides all things needed for you.

Study Questions

(1) What does living a "so what" kind of life look like?

(2) What 3 phrases help you to live a "so what" kind of life?

(3) If the gospel changes everything, how has it changed you and how does that provide you with encouragement?

(4) How specifically can you exercise your faith this week to live the abundant and fulfilling life scripture talks about? John 10:10b, John 6:35, Matthew 11:28–30, and Romans 8:32.

(5) In John 4, we see Jesus interacting with the woman at the well. What was Jesus saying to the woman? Who represents our rest?

(6) What does the doctrine of the preservation or perseverance of the saints mean? How does it provide a sinner with encouragement? How does it encourage you?

Chapter 3

For His Name Sake

"He leads me in paths of righteousness for his name's sake..."
Psalm 23:3b

In the previous chapter, we considered the restoration Christ, the Good Shepherd, offers and how life with him is better than anything else. As we move on in this Psalm, we are presented with the concept of sanctification, the process whereby we become more like him. Jesus, when he called his disciples, said: "Follow me, and I will make you become fishers of men" (Mark 1:17). Christ was promising to make them into something greater than themselves. They fished for fish. Now, they would fish for men.

Paul, in his letter to the Ephesians, says: "For we are his workmanship, created in Christ Jesus for good works, which God prepared beforehand, that we should walk in them" (Eph 2:10). Paul tells us that we were created for good works in Christ. If he created us for these good works, not that we should struggle in them because we cannot do them. But notice the ease of how he created us to attack these good works: "that we should *walk* in them." He will not give us a work we cannot do. That doesn't mean the result will be what we want or expect. But we will be able to do it.

When we look at the extent to which he restores our soul, the extent to which he pursues us when we are lost or have gone astray, the extent to which he provides all things, the road he leads us down—a narrow road that is difficult or appears thus, he does so faithfully and surely. As Paul reminds us, he will complete the work he has begun in us from before the foundations of the world (Eph 1:3-10; Phil 1:6). And again, this work is what we should walk in (Eph 2:10). In Adam, we found the certainty of death, sin, and destruction. In Christ, we find the certainty of life, righteousness, and preservation.

The first promise we see in Psalm 23, coming out of his restoration of our soul, is that he will lead us in paths of righteousness. David writes this in Psalm 57:2: "I cry out to God Most High, to God who fulfills his purpose for me." Then again, in Psalm 138:8: "The LORD will fulfill his purpose for me; your steadfast love, O LORD, endures forever. Do not forsake the work of your hands." Your steadfast love, O Lord, steadfast in all things, that love will fulfill your purpose in me.

Paul was as sure of this as David when he wrote in Philippians 1:6: "And I am sure of this, that he who began a good work in you will bring it to completion at the day of Jesus Christ." Also, in 1 Corinthians 1:4–9a: "I give thanks to my God always for you because of the grace of God that was given you in Christ Jesus, that in every way you were enriched in him in all speech and all knowledge—even as the testimony about Christ was confirmed among you—so that you are not lacking in any gift, as you wait for the revealing of our Lord Jesus Christ, who will sustain you to the end, guiltless in the day of our Lord Jesus Christ. God is faithful..."

What is the value in this? There is value in all things in righteousness. Psalm 19:7-10 reminds us: "The law of the LORD is perfect, reviving the soul; the testimony of the LORD is sure, making wise the simple; the precepts of the LORD are right, rejoicing the heart; the commandment of the LORD is pure, enlightening the eyes; the fear of the LORD is clean, enduring forever; the rules of the LORD are true, and righteous altogether. More to be desired are they than gold, even much fine gold; sweeter also than honey and drippings of the honeycomb. Moreover, by them is your servant warned; in keeping them is great reward." Psalm 119:1–7 declares this: "Blessed are those whose way is blameless, who walk in the law of the LORD! Blessed are those who keep his testimonies, who seek him with their whole heart, who also do no wrong, but walk in his ways! You have commanded your precepts to be kept diligently. Oh that my ways may be steadfast in keeping your statutes! Then I shall not be put to shame, having my eyes fixed on all your commandments. I will praise you with an upright heart, when I learn your righteous rules."

The path he leads us on is a narrow one. The narrow way may not be the easy way; it might be difficult. But the narrow way is the righteous way, the better way. It is more valuable than the pursuit of gold. Gold cannot buy joy or purpose or eternal life. Value? Faith in Christ that produces fruit and eternal life, that is a thing of value. His word guides, leads, and refreshes, keeping us from fainting or falling away.

What is the reason or purpose of our salvation and sanctification? The reason and purpose for our salvation and sanctification is for his glory and our enjoyment of him. He does it for his name's sake to preserve and demonstrate his character. We may be fallen but he redeems and restores.

Listen to what David says in others Psalms. "*For your name's sake*, O LORD, pardon my guilt, for it is great. Who is the man who fears the LORD? Him will he instruct in the way that he should choose" (Psalm 25:11–12). "For you are my rock and my fortress; and *for your name's sake* you lead me and guide me" (Psalm 31:3). Notice the repetition of the words "for your name's sake." This is the hinge of the door for the Psalm as it swings from promise to promise.

How does it show the sweetness and hope of the gospel? There is great hope and promise within this part of Psalm 23, for in it, we have the preservation of the saints. You see, he promises to lead us, keep us, hold us in paths of righteousness for his name's sake. He guarantees that those who are his, though they might fall into temptation or sin, though they might bring disgrace to the name of Christian, if Christ has called them, they will remain in faith, saved, and find grace and mercy in a saving God.

As I taught this point in Sunday school once, I emphasized the phrase "for his name's sake" repeatedly. Those in the class thought that I was being a bit absurd. They asked why this was so key. I reminded them of the dream given to Abraham in Genesis 15. The smoking fire pot dream pictures for us that when God makes a promise, he keeps it. His nature will not allow him to do otherwise. As a result, we can rest in that phrase for our eternity depends on it. For his name's sake!

J. I. Packer wrote: "Scripture emphasizes this. John tells us that Jesus Christ, the Good Shepherd, is under promise to his Father and to his sheep directly to keep them so that they never perish...Elsewhere he {Paul} rejoices in the certainty that God will complete the 'good work' that he began in the lives of those Paul addresses."[1]

Understand this from what is stated here in Psalm 23 and elsewhere—God is the one who is preserving the elect. Notice the language: "He *leads* me in paths of righteousness for his name sake."

The Westminster Confession of Faith says the following: "They, whom God has accepted in his beloved, effectually called, and sanctified by his Spirit, can neither totally nor finally fall away from the state of grace, but shall certainly persevere therein to the end, and be eternally saved."

The character of God guarantees these promises. It is not based on me or my work, thank goodness. Instead, the basis for the promise keeping is in the name of the Lord, who is all holy and perfect. Scripture is in agreement on this point.

Let's tour through the Old and New Testaments to get a sampling of this.

- Isaiah 43:1-3: "But now thus says the LORD, he who created you, O Jacob, he who formed you, O Israel: "Fear not, for I have redeemed you; I have called you by name, you are mine. When you pass through the waters, I will be with you; and through the rivers, they shall not overwhelm you; when you walk through fire you shall not be burned, and the flame shall not consume you. *For I am the LORD your God, the Holy One of Israel, your Savior.*"

- Isaiah 54:10: "'For the mountains may depart and the hills be removed, but my steadfast love shall not depart from you, and my covenant of peace shall not be removed,' says the LORD, *who has compassion on you.*"

- Matthew 18:12-14: "What do you think? If a man has a hundred sheep, and one of them has gone astray, does he not leave the ninety-nine on the mountains and go in search of the one that went astray? And if he finds it, truly, I say to you, he rejoices over it more than over the ninety-nine that never went astray. *So it is not the will of my Father who is in heaven that one of these little ones should perish."*

- John 6:37–40: "*All that the Father gives me will come to me, and whoever comes to me I will never cast out.* For I have come down from heaven, not to do my own will but the will of him who sent me. And this is the will of him who sent me, that I should lose nothing of all that he has given me, but raise it up on the last day. For this is the will of my Father, that everyone who looks on the Son and believes in him should have eternal life, and I will raise him up on the last day."

- John 10:27–30: "My sheep hear my voice, and I know them, and they follow me. I give them eternal life, and they will never perish, and no one will snatch them out of my hand. *My Father, who has given them to me, is greater than all, and no one is able to snatch them out of the Father's hand.* I and the Father are one."

- John 17:11–12, 15: "And I am no longer in the world, but they are in the world, and I am coming to you. Holy Father, *keep them in your name,* which you have given me, that they may be one, even as we are one.

While I was with them, *I kept them in your name*, which you have given me. *I have guarded them*, and not one of them has been lost except the son of destruction, that the Scripture might be fulfilled...I do not ask that you take them out of the world, but that you keep them from the evil one."

- 1 Corinthians 1:4-9: "I give thanks to my God always for you because of the grace of God that was given you in Christ Jesus, that in every way you were enriched in him in all speech and all knowledge— even as the testimony about Christ was confirmed among you— so that you are not lacking in any gift, as you wait for the revealing of our Lord Jesus Christ, who will sustain you to the end, guiltless in the day of our Lord Jesus Christ. *God is faithful*, by whom you were called into the fellowship of his Son, Jesus Christ our Lord."

- Philippians 1:6: "And I am sure of this, that *he who began a good work in you will bring it to completion* at the day of Jesus Christ."

- 1 Thessalonians 5:23-24: "Now may the God of peace himself sanctify you completely, and may your whole spirit and soul and body be kept blameless at the coming of our Lord Jesus Christ. *He who calls you is faithful; he will surely do it.*"

- Hebrews 3:6: "...but *Christ is faithful over God's house* as a son. And we are his house, if indeed we hold fast our confidence and our boasting in our hope."

- 1 Peter 1:3-5: "Blessed be the God and Father of our Lord Jesus Christ! According to his great mercy, *he has caused us to be born again* to a living hope through the resurrection of Jesus Christ from the dead, to an inheritance that is imperishable, undefiled, and unfading, kept in heaven for you, who *by God's power are being guarded through faith* for a salvation ready to be revealed in the last time."

- Jude 1, 24, 25: "Jude, a servant of Jesus Christ and brother of James, To those who are called, beloved in God the Father and kept for Jesus Christ...*Now to him who is able* to keep you from stumbling and to present you blameless before the presence of his glory with great joy, to the only God, our Savior, through Jesus Christ our Lord, be glory, majesty, dominion, and authority, before all time and now and forever. Amen."

Do you now see the incredible surety of "for his name sake?" Do you see the omnipotence brimming out of it? Do you feel and see the force of it when Jesus said that heaven and earth might pass away but my words will not (Matthew 24:35)? Jesus is able and he will do it. He will hold your past, present, and future and will never let it go. He will redeem it, wipe away the tears, and make all things right—for his name sake.

What, then, should be our response? 1 Peter 1:6-9: "In this you rejoice, though now for a little while, if necessary, you have been grieved by various trials, so that the tested genuineness of your faith—more precious than gold that perishes though it is tested by fire—may be found to result in praise and glory and honor at the revelation of Jesus Christ. *Though you have not seen him, you love him. Though you do not now see him, you believe in him and rejoice with joy that is inexpressible and filled with glory, obtaining the outcome of your faith, the salvation of your souls.*"

This doesn't mean that everyone who professes faith will be saved. False professions are made and many fall away. Jesus reminds us of this in his Parable of the Sower in Matthew 13. We see this displayed with the seed sown on rocky and weed soils. But not only there, Jesus provides what is probably one of the most frightening passages in Scripture in Matthew 7, when he says: "Not everyone who says to me, 'Lord, Lord,' will enter the kingdom of heaven, but the one who does the will of my Father who is in heaven. On that day many will say to me, 'Lord, Lord, did we not prophesy in your name, and cast out demons in your name, and do many mighty works in your name?' And then will I declare to them, 'I never knew you; depart from me, you workers of lawlessness.'"

To understand this warning better, here are some helpful hints. When a name is repeated twice, it is not for emphasis, rather it implies a relationship. Those who say "Lord, Lord" and don't enter the kingdom of God thought that they had a relationship with him and, indeed, might have seemed like it on the outside. But we see quickly what the basis of their faith was comprised. They say: "Did we not prophesy...did we not cast out demons...did we not do many mighty works..." What are they basing their salvation on? They are basing it on their works and deeds. They rested not in the saving grace and mercy of the Lord Jesus Christ but in their effort. Even though they stated it was done in "his name," it is clear from the tone and the language that they were doing it for their own glory, name, and praise.

So, what is the will of God the Father? John 6:40 reminds us: "For this is the will of my Father, that everyone who looks on the Son and believes in him should have eternal life, and I will raise him up on the last day." What does that life of faith lead to? Doing the good work that he created for you to do from the foundation of the world for his glory alone. That is our chief end. Spurgeon wrote: "And as from him we live, so for him we live, if we live aright. We wish so to act as to glorify God in everything. Even our salvation should not be an ultimate end with any one of us; we should desire to glorify God by our salvation."[2]

Do not miss the sweetness of this part of the Psalm. It is the hinge that holds the door of your past, present, and future. He will keep us and hold us throughout our lives as he makes us lie down, leads us beside still waters, and restores us. He will keep us and hold us as we go through the valley of the shadow of death. He will keep us and hold us as he welcomes us to his table in glory. In it, we find security, rest, and peace. As the familiar hymn goes:

Verse 1:

Be still, my soul; the Lord is on thy side;
bear patiently the cross of grief or pain.
Leave to thy God to order and provide;
in every change He faithful will remain.
Be still, my soul; thy best, thy heav'nly Friend
through thorny ways leads to a joyful end.
Verse 2:

Be still, my soul; thy God doth undertake
to guide the future as He has the past.
Thy hope, thy confidence let nothing shake;
all now mysterious shall be bright at last.
Be still, my soul; the waves and winds still know
His voice who ruled them while He dwelt below.

Verse 3:

Be still, my soul; when dearest friends depart,
and all is darkened in the veil of tears,
then shalt thou better know His love, His heart,
who comes to soothe thy sorrow and thy fears.
Be still, my soul; thy Jesus can repay
from His own fullness all He takes away.

Verse 4:

Be still, my soul; the hour is hast'ning on
when we shall be forever with the Lord,
when disappointment, grief, and fear are gone,

sorrow forgot, love's purest joys restored.
Be still, my soul; when change and tears are past,
all safe and blessed we shall meet at last.3

Study Questions

(1) What is the significance of the phrase "for his name sake?" Psalm 25:11–12, Psalm 31:3

(2) What does it mean that his character guarantees our sanctification? Isaiah 43:1–3, Isaiah 54:10, Matthew 18:12–14; John 6:37–40; John 10:27–30; John 17:11–12, 15; 1 Corinthians 1:4–9; Philippians 1:6; 1 Thessalonians 5:23–24; Hebrews 3:6; 1 Peter 1:3–5; Jude 1, 24, 25

(3) Does this negate our responsibility? How are you working with the Spirit to grow in your faith? Philippians 2:12

(4) How do you respond to the gospel in your life? 1 Peter 1:6–9

(5) What should you base your faith on? What do you base your faith on? Where do you need to change your perspective? Matthew 13:1–9, Matthew 7:21–23, Matthew 25:31–46

(6) What hymns inspire and encourage you in the paths of righteousness?

Chapter 4

His Love Endures Forever

"Give thanks to the Lord, for he is good, for his steadfast love endures forever." Psalm 136:1

Canute the Great ruled England during the early 11th Century. Throughout his reign, those in his court were quick to praise and flatter him. In their flattery, they even went as far as to say that his power was unstoppable and that all things would be obedient to his command. Canute, knowing that they had gone too far, is said to have taken the following method to correct them. He ordered his throne to be placed on the sea shore as the tide was coming in. He then sat down and commanded the waves to stop coming in and for the tide to go out. He was heard to say this: "You are under my dominion. The land upon which I sit is mine. I charge you, therefore, to approach no further, nor dare to wet the feet of your sovereign." He feigned to sit some time in expectation. You can just imagine how uncomfortable all of the nobles were. Eventually, the waves completely surrounded the chair at which point Canute turned and said this: "The titles of Lord and Master belong only to him whom both earth and seas were ready to obey."[1]

As we contemplate this idea of "for his name sake," consider with me this song of worship from Psalm 136. Behind every refrain is "for his name sake." It represents the perfect picture of the Lord's steadfast love for his people. We see with each line a glimpse of David as he rested in the One who held his past, present, and future. We come face to face with the grace, mercy, and love of God as history is played out. We are confronted with the God of our past, present, and future. The question is, how will we respond to God's endless love?

As I worked through this passage and read it again and again, my mind turned to a time in my life when a great tragedy struck. My father was diagnosed with cancer and would die 5 years later. I lost my job. To top everything off, for 30 years, I suffered from chronic pain. For 20 years of that, there wasn't a moment of a day without pain. I took upwards of 2000 pills a year just to dull it enough for me to function. These were nothing compared to the day when we were told our son would not live. He would not live through the pregnancy. He would die a painful and horrible death. The advice they gave was to abort his life and move on. I remember driving to work after that visit, and what a miracle it was that I made it because of the tears. I had never cried so hard. The pain was crushing. This was my son. I remember at one point taking a walk and praying and saying to God: "I don't know what you are doing but I trust you and know you will take care of my family." I spent many nights talking with dear friends from the church. Through it all, I learned a difficult lesson: as hard as it is, as painful as it might get, if the gospel is true, then I must learn to trust in him. I must rest in the One who holds my past, present, and future.

If all good news begins with Christ and apart from him, there is no good news, then I must be able to find the gospel even in tragedy. And, I found it. If God decided to take my son, then I knew I would have an eternity of memories with him in heaven. For I know whom I have believed and am convinced that he is able to keep that which I have entrusted to him to that day. If God decided to let my son live, then I knew I would have a lifetime of memories with him here and knew that when he came to faith would lead to an eternity of memories with him in heaven.

I could easily write this Psalm, putting my story into it and so could you. We would see the same points: He is the God of our past, our present, and our future. And, we would also see the same refrain: the Lord's steadfast love endures forever. Just like the Israelites, I can look back with confidence and say that refrain over and over. Can you? In all of the trials, in all of the heartache, in all situations, I see the goodness of God and His love working it out for my good. This is what the Psalm is doing. It is recentering our thinking, recentering our focus. The more we look at this Psalm, the more we realize that it is centered on God, not Israel. Despite the history lesson, the Psalm is about God and his endless love. And that is where we find the main point of this passage.

"Give thanks to the Lord, for he is good, for his steadfast love endures forever. Give thanks to the God of gods, for his steadfast love endures forever. Give thanks to the Lord of lords, for his steadfast love endures forever." David tells us that the object of our worship, the object of our thanksgiving, the object of our praise is Jehovah, the God of gods and Lord of lords (verses 1–3).

Notice the repetition. Threefold he tells us to give thanks

to the LORD and, in doing so, he puts emphasis on who we are to worship...and that we are to worship him and him alone. Throughout the rest of Psalm, David labors to show us why we should worship him by pointing to who he is and what he has done for us. Look at how this is played out.

- He created all things, sustains all things by his mighty hand (Ps 136:4-9).

- He led Israel out of bondage, out of Egypt (Psalm 136:10-16).

- He planted Israel in the land of promise (Psalm 136:17-22).

- He remembers and demonstrates in all things his faithfulness (Psalm 136:23).

- He rescues us from our bondage (Psalm 136:24).

- He provides for our needs (Psalm 136:25).

- He provides for our future (Psalm 136:26).

He is the God of our past, present, and future. In the midst of this realization, David calls us to worship the Lord and him only. This is not the only place in scripture where we are called in this manner. In Exodus 20: "I am the LORD your God, who brought you out of the land of Egypt, out of the house of slavery. You shall have no other gods before me... You shall not make for yourself a carved image... you shall not bow down to them or serve them... You shall not take the name of the LORD your God in vain." Again, in Matthew 6: "Our Father in heaven, hallowed be your name. Your kingdom come, your will be done, on earth as it is in heaven."

The principles we see here in the "who" of worship are these. First, we are not to have any other gods in his presence. Second, we are to serve God alone. Third, we are to honor and glorify his name. It is not about your rights or mine. It is about his honor and glory.

The call, therefore, is to worship the God of Creation. We worship the God of our past. We give thanks to the One who has proven his power and sovereignty over all things, who has held us graciously in His hand. We not only give thanks but we remember what he has done. After all, that is what giving thanks involves—remembering. Remembering is integral to thanksgiving.

Remembering was the primary call of Moses to the people of Israel as he gave his farewell address in Deuteronomy. He said over and over: "Remember!" Why?

Because we easily forget! We need to remember that God is infinitely worthy of worship and glory. We must not forget it or lose sight of it. There is none like him. Everything was made by him, and we should praise and thank him for his graciousness toward us in providing all things. Nothing came about by accident but is full of perfect order, design, and purpose.

We see all of this in the passage: "to him who alone does great wonders...to him who by understanding made the heavens...to him who spread out the earth above the waters...to him who made the great lights...the sun to rule over the day...the moon and stars to rule over the night." Indeed, all of creation should cause us to pause and give him praise and worship and glory.

He is the God of Creation. He is the God of our Past. He is a Great and Mighty God who alone deserves to be worshipped. He is also the God of Salvation. He is the God of our Present. We see from this passage that God is a rescuer who sees us in our distress. David talks about this, giving the example of the people of Israel, imprisoned by Pharoah, set free through Moses. He details this not just to give a history lesson but to remind them that their identity and reason for hope can be found in him.

Ephesians 2 tells us that we are dead in sin, freed and made alive in Christ. Ephesians 5 tells us that we are now children of light. Over and over again, scripture reminds us of our identity in him.

When I was 10 months old, my biological father died. When I was 2 years old, I was adopted. I got a new birth certificate with a new name. On it was the name of my new father. All of a sudden, I had an identity rooted in my father.

Why is it important to see this not just as a history lesson but as your identity? It changes how you live! How does seeing our identity in Him change how we live? Galatians 5 reminds us that it is "for freedom Christ has set us free; stand firm therefore, and do not submit again to a yoke of slavery." The Parable of the Sower states rather clearly that all good soil produces fruit. Exodus 20 reminds us that our identity is in him; that we are His people and He is our God; and that our actions should follow that identity. In each of these, we are told that our identity drives how we live. Indeed, the mighty God of Salvation is at work in you for his name sake so you can pursue obedience. He has indeed remembered us in our low estate. He still sees us now. He still rescues us. He is the God of Salvation. He is the redeemer and rescuer who alone deserves to be worshipped.

Finally, he is the God of Heaven—our hope and future. Philippians 1 reminds us that the God who has carried us thus far will carry us to the end. Because of this, we have hope for the future. Hebrews 12 talks about this promise and hope for the future. The author of Hebrews says this: "At that time his voice shook the earth, but now he has promised, 'Yet once more I will shake not only the earth but also the heavens.' This phrase, 'Yet once more,' indicates the removal of things that are shaken—that is, things that have been made—in order that the things that cannot be shaken may remain. Therefore let us be grateful for receiving a kingdom that cannot be shaken, and thus let us offer to God acceptable worship, with reverence and awe, for our God is a consuming fire" (Hebrews 12:26–29).

So, what are the things that cannot be shaken? When I was a child, Dr. Charles Stanley preached a sermon on this passage. He noted four things that should drive us to our knees in worship. First, the LORD. He cannot be shaken. He is the one doing the shaking. Second, God's word. It endures forever. It is trustworthy. Third, our relationship with him.

Jesus encouraged us and reminded us that when the Father takes ahold of us, nothing can shake us loose from his grip as he is greater than all things. Fourth, our future home with him.[2] He is the God of Heaven, our hope and future. Praise his name!

And so, we worship and praise God with all of who we are. This is what we need to remember; this is what we drill into our heads and hearts with repetition. This is how we interpret our stories—the steadfast love of our God is everlasting. From that repetition, we seek to love him more than we love anything else, to know him more than we know anything else, to treasure him more than we treasure anything else, and to seek after him more than we seek after anything. For he alone is worthy of praise and worship. We do not consider it tiring; we do not consider it to be a chore to come to worship; we do not consider it boring. But rather we find our joy, our strength, our renewal, and our hope in him and him alone.

Before we move back into Psalm 23, let's consider a couple of points implied in this passage that are helpful to us in the act of worship.

First, with whom should we worship. When I was a little

child, some of my earliest memories were in church. Every time there was a recitation or liturgy read and every time there was a hymn sung, I remember my father kneeling at my side, pointing at each word spoken and at each word sung. He did not allow me to bring anything to church that would distract me but had me sit with either mom or him to learn and pay attention. All of this to teach me that (1) I had a place in the service, even as a little one; (2) I had a role in the service, the same as his; (3) that my attention belonged to God; (4) God was the most important; and (5) he cared enough to take an active role in making sure I saw it.

As I grew up, this manifested itself in 5:15 am family devotions five days a week. I can't say I liked those as I am not a morning person. But, I remember them. I remember the discipline, the order, the purpose, and the prayer.

So, what does this have to do with this Psalm? What does this have to do with Psalm 23? The Psalm is meant as a recitation, meaning it was meant to be read in community. Who are we to worship with, all for the glory of God? The answer: each other. Yes, the fellowship of believers is important. The author of Hebrews says in chapter 10: "Let us not give up meeting together, as some are in the habit of doing, but let us encourage one another – and all the more as you see the Day approaching." Psalm 23 is about sheep among sheep. It is not about the shepherd just taking out one sheep at a time. Life was meant to be lived by grace through faith in community.

I remember when my daughter, Victoria, was an infant, I sang in the church choir. You know, the kind with robes. Every Sunday, Victoria was with me. While I sang, I held her. While I sat, I held her. She slept on me the whole time. It was a humorous sight but I remember the pastor one day commenting on the sight of it, the beauty of it.

So, what does this have to do with this Psalm? Our worship was not just meant to be together but to include everyone. This recitation from Psalm 136 was easy and, therefore, designed for even young ones to participate in and learn, just like hymns and songs are meant to be easy, repetitive, and storytelling. This Psalm reminds us that our worship is not just meant for adults but for the little children as well.

Second, how should we worship. Within each verse of the Psalm, we see a call and response. The Psalm is participatory. Relationship with God is not something we watch or spectate. Hebrews 12 reminds us that we run a race. Ephesians 6 tells us to put on the armor of God and fight. The Psalm is simple, so much so that young and old can understand it. And yet, it is truly profound; His love is proven in the past, carries us now, and will carry us in the future. The Psalm is repetitive. The truths we most want to know need to be repeated—the covenant fidelity of God. His faithful love is our heritage and legacy. He was our God in the past, He will be our God in the future. He will not abandon us now (Ps 94:14); His Kingdom is forever. And we worship him, praising his name with passion.

Notice how Moses sings praise to God for his steadfast love, for holding his past, present, and future, and for his gracious provision in all things. Notice how Moses sees that the victories he experienced were of God and not him. Notice how God was doing it "for his name sake." This was the song Moses wrote after God's redemption of his people in Exodus 15: "'I will sing to the LORD, for he has triumphed gloriously; the horse and his rider he has thrown into the sea. The LORD is my strength and my song, and he has become my salvation; this is my God, and I will praise him, my father's God, and I will exalt him. The LORD is a man of war; the LORD is his name.'" "Who is like you, O LORD, among the gods? Who is like you, majestic in holiness, awesome in glorious deeds, doing wonders? You stretched out your right hand; the earth swallowed them. "You have led in your steadfast love the people whom you have redeemed; you have guided them by your strength to your holy abode" (Exodus 15:1–3, 11–13).

Will you praise his name today to tell of his steadfast love? What will it say? What does it say about who you belong to?

Study Questions

(1) Looking back on your life, how do you see God's hand guiding and directing your path? How does it inform how you live today? How does it inform how you prepare for tomorrow?

(2) When looking at your life, do you say with the Psalmist: "Your steadfast love endures forever" in all things?

(3) How does the steadfast love of the Lord change your perspective?

(4) What cannot be shaken? Hebrews 12:26–29 Why is this important to understanding that his love endures forever and that his promises are guaranteed for his name's sake?

Chapter 5

The Valley of the Shadow

"Even though I walk through the valley of the shadow of death, I will fear no evil, for you are with me; your rod and your staff, they comfort me." Psalm 23:4

Over the years, I have come to grasp the beauty of the gospel. More than finding forgiveness and newness in life, I have found contentment no matter the circumstance. Even facing death or the prospect of it, I find myself calm and surprisingly ok. It truly hit me when I was flying from Charlotte to somewhere through Phoenix. I was in first class and had fallen asleep. As the plane was approaching its connecting location, all of a sudden there was a tremendous amount of hustle and bustle. Flight attendants were walking the cabin through emergency procedures. All the while, I was slowly waking up. As we began the descent, the pilot came over the intercom and declared: "Get into crash position. Prepare for multiple impacts." Really? Like the first wouldn't be bad enough? In that moment, there was no panic.

There was no worry. There were no tears. The things that I used to fear and hate—flying and death—no longer scared me. After we landed safely, the entire cabin erupted in applause. I was ok no matter the outcome.

Why was I ok in the face of death? Why was I not scared? I think for this reason, the gospel, as found in this Psalm, tells us that, as Christians, we have nothing to fear, even in the face of death. Throughout this chapter, I will be quoting frequently from Charles Spurgeon's sermons. His insights into a Christian's perspective on death are truly transformative.

As I consider verse 4, there are eight certainties that I see that will, if taken to heart, change not only how you think but how you live and die. My father, as I watched him die, taught me not just how to live but how to die as well. Within that lesson, I see these eight certainties in verse 4:

(1) That, until he comes back, we will see the valley of the shadow of death.

(2) That if we are his, for his name's sake, we will have life eternal.

(3) That death is merely a door that leads to life for those found in him.

(4) That in the face of death, for those in Christ, there is no fear but rather peace.

(5) That we have that peace precisely because he is with us.

(6) That we know he will never leave us or forsake us.

(7) That his character is proven by his word.

(8) That his word (his rod and staff) is a source of comfort in all things everywhere.

If you recall, at the beginning of this book, I said this Psalm was about Christ for the encouragement of Christians. As we watch Jesus in the gospels going through the valley of the shadow of death, he took comfort in the fact that his Father was there. In the garden after the Last Supper, while he was being beaten during the trial, as the nails were being driven into his hands and feet at the crucifixion, he cried out: "Father, forgive them" and "Into your hands do I commit my spirit." He took comfort, as he quoted from the Psalms, hanging on the tree. Because of him, we can say: "When the perishable puts on the imperishable, and the mortal puts on immortality, then shall come to pass the saying that is written: 'Death is swallowed up in victory.' 'O death, where is your victory? O death, where is your sting?'" (1 Corinthians 15:54–55).

When we think of death, we think of heaven. When we think of heaven, we think of God the Father who holds us. We think of the Son who prepares a place for us. We think of the Spirit who seals the promise, ensuring we get there. Spurgeon, in his sermon on John 17, said: "Yes, all our steps are towards the Father. We are saved when by believing in the name of Jesus we receive power to become the sons of God. Our sanctification lies in the bosom of our adoption. Because Jesus comes from the Father and leads us back to the Father, therefore is there a heaven for us. Wherefore, whenever we think of heaven let us chiefly think of the Father; for it is in our Father's house that there are many mansions, and it is to the Father that our Lord as gone, that he may prepare a place for us."[1] We can, therefore, rejoice even in the face of death for eternity has been secured for his name sake.

Just as we have the confidence of the believer being, "I shall not want," we have the courage of the believer as he faces death with "I will fear no evil." The courage of the believer says: "I will fear no evil" as he looks back on life, seeing the goodness of God in all things. Seeing what God has done in verses 1–3, the believer's confidence is bolstered as he moves into the shadow. His confidence remains unshaken with a firm reliance on the one who said he would be there for the promise was guaranteed by his character.

With that in mind, let's consider the first certainty: until he comes back, we will see the valley of the shadow of death. I love what Spurgeon wrote: "We dwell in a poor uncomfortable tent; continually is the canvas being rent, the cords are being loosed, and the tent pins are being pulled up. We are full of sufferings, and aches, and pains, which are but the premonitions of coming death."[2] Being a Christian does not exempt us from pain, suffering, or death. It doesn't exempt us from trials. These we will see in this life.

However, the difference between Christians and non-Christians is in how they view death. First, for Christians, there is no difference between one's outlook in life, whether old or young. Going from being led and laying down and being restored, the psalmist says, "even though." Whether old or young, sick or healthy, strong or weak, blind or with sight, the Lord was still his shepherd. In that place, he was content. In that place, I am content as well. Even though I find myself old, infirm, and dying, the Lord is still my shepherd. I find my path in him. I find my security in him. I find my comfort in him.

Second, unlike the non-Christian, the believer doesn't see death as death but rather a shadow, for it holds no power or sting. This is what Paul reminded the Corinthians. There is something beyond death that is life eternal. That is the story of the gospel. Christ came to live the perfect life that we could not so that he could pay the penalty for sin that we deserved so that he could rise again and ascend to heaven conquering death and ensuring our eternal life with him.

This is a critical point. Because of the person and work of Christ, death is not death but a mere shadow. A shadow does nothing when you walk into it. We walk through shadows every day. There is no sting. They do not hurt. This is the point the psalmist is making. In light of eternity, there is no victory in death. You walk "through" the shadow into the sun. You enter into the presence of the Son.

For the unbeliever, death is a permanent suffering—a sting, a defeat with no end. A Christian walks through the shadow. A non-Christian is lost in the shadow. Without a Good Shepherd to take them through, the non-Christian suffers an eternity of loss. It is a curse upon curse. This is why there is an urgency for the gospel to be made known. Without Christ, there is no hope for eternity, only curse.

This brings me to my second certainty: that if we are his, for his name's sake, we will have life eternal. Spurgeon wrote: "Jesus never so prays for the whole church as to forget a single member; neither does he so pray for the members individually as to overlook the corporate capacity of the whole. Sweet thought! Jesus wills to have the whole of what he bought with his precious blood with him in heaven; he will not lose any part. He did not die for a part of a church, nor will he be satisfied unless the entire flock which he has purchased shall be gathered around him."[3]

The promise of Psalm 23:4 is what comes afterward—eternal life. We see in the following verses the banquet table that is spread in front of us, the anointing, the blessing, the dwelling. These are the promises of the life to come and we live to bring honor and glory to him in this life for it. This is the promise of the gospel, this is the hope we have: Christ in you, the hope of glory (Col 1:27). The triple blessing and guarantee: we are his and he is ours, because Jesus and the Father are one, we are his too. We are a gift from the Father to the Son. All that he gave the Son will never be lost. His character guarantees it.

Did you hear that? His character guarantees it. For his name's sake, now do you see the power of that phrase? Praise be to his name! Not one will be lost. Once he has you in his grip, no one, nothing, can ever pry you loose from his hand. No one, nothing, can separate you from his love. We are his and have eternal life. And so, we say with Paul: "But whatever gain I had, I counted as loss for the sake of Christ. Indeed, I count everything as loss because of the surpassing worth of knowing Christ Jesus my Lord. For his sake I have suffered the loss of all things and count them as rubbish, in order that I may gain Christ and be found in him, not having a righteousness of my own that comes from the law, but that which comes through faith in Christ, the righteousness from God that depends on faith—that I may know him and the power of his resurrection, and may share his sufferings, becoming like him in his death, that by any means possible I may attain the resurrection from the dead" (Phil 3:7–11).

The third certainty I find is this: death is merely a door that leads to life for those found in him. Spurgeon wrote: "To them (Christians), it is not death to die; it is a departure out of this world unto the Father, a being unclothed that we may be clothed upon, a falling asleep, an entrance into the Kingdom."[4]

Paul put this point this way in Philippians 1:21: "For to me to live is Christ, and to die is gain. If I am to live in the flesh, that means fruitful labor for me. Yet which I shall choose I cannot tell. I am hard pressed between the two. My desire is to depart and be with Christ, for that is far better. But to remain in the flesh is more necessary on your account." For the Christian, death is not a thing to be dreaded or feared, but a door to eternal life that we must pass. Paul calls it gain. I love how Spurgeon put it: "a being unclothed..." All of my decay, pain, and suffering, when I pass through the valley of the shadow of death, get unclothed and replaced with a new body that will not decay. How could I not look forward to that? How could I view death as anything but a door from mortality to immortality, from curse to blessing?

For the non-Christian, though, this is a door from curse to curse, from decay in this life to everlasting decay in the next (Mark 9:48). Christ says it is a door to hell where the worm never dies and the fire is never quenched. Dear friend, if you do not know the blessing of the gospel and the pleasantness of the Good Shepherd, come to the gate and he will receive you. Scripture is clear, there is only one way to heaven and eternal life—Jesus Christ. All other ways lead to hell and eternal death. Do not be misled on this point.

This leads me to my fourth certainty: in the face of death, for those in Christ, there is no fear but rather peace. Spurgeon wrote: "Death, then, does not come to me as a believer because I deserve it and must be punished by it; it comes so to the ungodly, it is upon them a fit visitation for their iniquities, the beginning of an unending death, which shall be their perpetual portion. To the saints, the sting of death is gone, and the victory of the grave is removed; it is no more a penalty but a privilege to die... To fall asleep in Jesus is a blessing of the covenant; it is a grace to be asked for, 'Lord, now let your servant depart in peace according to your word.'"[5]

Because we are his and he is ours, because of the person and work of the Good Shepherd, because of the character of God that secures our place with him by grace through faith, because he has gone before us and leads us, keeping us to the end, because of this, we do not fear death. We view it no differently than life. We see it as a stepping stone from here to there, as a mere shadow. There is no fear in the shadow because the light of the Son is on the other side. Paul writes in Philippians 3:12-16 the following as an encouragement to all of us as we move through this life: "Not that I have already obtained this or am already perfect, but I press on to make it my own, because Christ Jesus has made me his own. Brothers, I do not consider that I have made it my own. But one thing I do: forgetting what lies behind and straining forward to what lies ahead, I press on toward the goal for the prize of the upward call of God in Christ Jesus. Let those of us who are mature think this way, and if in anything you think otherwise, God will reveal that also to you. Only let us hold true to what we have attained."

The fifth certainty flows from the fourth: we have that peace precisely because he is with us. Spurgeon wrote: "Still, the surest method of getting rid of present tears, is communion and fellowship with God. When I can creep under the wing of my dear God and nestle close to his bosom, let the world say what it will, and let the devil roar as he pleases, and let my sins accuse and threaten as they may, I am safe, content, happy, peaceful, rejoicing.

"Let earth against my soul engage,
And hellish darts be hurled;
Now can I smile at Satan's rage,
And face a frowning world."[6]

We have peace, and we have victory precisely because he is with us. Picture with me David, a type of Christ. For 40 days, Goliath frightened the people of Israel into a corner. Where was the champion of the people, King Saul? The one they wanted? Hiding in his tent, trembling in fear. David, hearing the calls of the evil one, came to fight. Standing in the gap for his people, David was confident and at peace, knowing victory was his because God was with him.

Fast forward to the desert temptation of Christ in Matthew 4. Jesus had been there for 40 days, fasting and praying. The evil one came to tempt him. What did Jesus do? Rested in his Father. He stood in the gap and fought to succeed where Adam failed. "Thus saith the Lord," Jesus said time and again. The sword of the Spirit was drawn. Fighting as we should, knowing victory belongs to the Father and defeat to the evil one.

Spurgeon wrote: "To say, 'My Father, God,' to put myself right into his hand, and feel that I am safe there; to look up to him though it be with tears in my eyes and feel that he loves me, and then to put my head right into his bosom as the prodigal did, and sob my griefs out there into my Father's heart, oh, this is the death of grief, and the life of all consolation. Is not Jehovah call the God of all comfort? You will find him so, beloved. He has been 'our help in ages past;' he is 'our hope for years to come.'"[7]

This is the picture we have here. If God is for us, who can be against us? Even if they take this body, they cannot touch the soul and victory is still mine. For there will come a day when the judgment of God comes and makes right what was wrong, restores what was broken, and redeems what was lost.

I remember hearing stories about the death of my grandfather. He was so dear to me that I could not bear the thought of losing him. I wept for months. Every time I spoke with him on the phone, I wept. My grandmother wrote to me afterward, knowing this. She told me of his death that he asked for the great hymns to be sung so that as he left this life into the next, it would be from this choir to the next. No fear, great peace. A readiness that says with Spurgeon: "Hail, messenger of the King! The sound of thy master's feet is behind thee; thou are welcome here, for thy Master sent thee."[8]

The sixth certainty rests in the promise of the phrase "for his name sake." We know he will never leave us or forsake us. Spurgeon wrote: "Precious promises are illustrated upon dying beds. 'I will never leave thee nor forsake thee.' Who would have known the meaning of that to the full, if he had not found that the Lord did not leave him when all else was gone? 'When thou passeth through the river I will be with thee.' Who could have known the depth of truth in that word, if saints did not pass through the last cold stream. 'As they days so shall thy strength be.' Who could have known to the full that word, if had not seen the believer triumphant on his dying day? 'Yea, though I pass through the valley of the shadow of death, I will fear no evil, for though are with me; thy rod and thy staff comfort me.' You may read commentaries upon that psalm, but you will never value it so well as when you are in the valley yourself."[9]

A beautiful picture of the grace and mercy of God through trials. Think of David as he writes in the Psalms: "Even if my mother and father forsake me, the Lord will never." See the picture here? There is nothing more horrible than a mother or father abandoning their child to death.

Why? They, of all people, should love that child, for they see themselves in that child.

Even more than that love of a mother and father, the Good Shepherd promises fidelity. Not one sheep will be lost. This is why Paul can be so confident throughout Romans 8: (1) there is now no condemnation for those in Christ, (2) we are more than conquerors through Christ, (3) nothing and no one can separate us from the love of the Father in Christ Jesus. David has these things in mind as he wrote Psalm 23. His confidence didn't wane. It waxed stronger with each moment of the valley of the shadow.

Why does it wax stronger with each moment is the seventh certainty: his character is proven by his word. The Lord is altogether consistent, righteous, and faithful. He is immutable, meaning he doesn't change. Even if we deny him like Peter did, even if we run away from him as did Jonah, even if we sin greatly against him as did David, he will always remain faithful because he cannot deny himself (2 Tim 2:11–13). If he said it, he will do it.

Spurgeon wrote: "More than intercession is found in the expression 'I will.' It suggests the idea of a testamentary bequest and appointment. The Lord Jesus is making his last will and testament, and he writes, 'Father, I will that they also, whom thou has given me, be with me.' No man who makes his will likes to have it frustrated. Our Savior's will assuredly be carried out in every jot and tittle; and, if for no other reason, yet certainly for this cause, that though he died, and thus made his will valid, yet he lives again to be his own executor, and to carry out his will."[10]

You want a good sense of this one? Spend time reading Psalm 119. David will tell you about the word of God and how God's character is proven true time and again, without fail. Not one "jot or tittle" will fail. All will come to pass as the Lord has decreed it to. It is not surprising that this is the longest chapter in the Bible. If we don't have confidence in this, how can we have confidence in the rest?

Finally, we have the eighth certainty: his word (his rod and staff) is a source of comfort in all things everywhere. Spurgeon wrote: "When with strong crying and tears he poured out his soul unto death, his Father granted the requests of his heart. I do not wonder it should be so; how could the best Beloved fail of that which he sought in intercession from his Father God! Mark, then, that the force of irresistible intercession is drawing every blood-bought soul into the place where Jesus is. You cannot hold you dying babe; for Jesus asks for it to be with him. Will you come into competition with your Lord? Surely you will not. You cannot hold your aged father, nor detain your beloved mother, beyond the time appointed; for the intersession of Christ has such a force about it that they must ascend even as sparks must seek the sun."[11]

The word of God is where Jesus found comfort on the cross. We hear him quoting from scripture (Psalm 22). Jesus was confident and comforted, knowing the Father's plan had succeeded. That is why he so confidently stated: "You don't take my life; I give it" (John 10:18). This is what gave Jesus comfort in the desert during the temptation. He said: "Man shall not live on bread alone but by every word that proceeds from the mouth of God" (Matt 4:1–11). This is why Jesus, even though he was wearied and hungry, was not distraught or dismayed when speaking with the woman at the well. Instead, to the amazement of the disciples, he said: "I have food that you know not of" (John 4). The word of God should be to us that same source of comfort and sustenance. It should sustain us from this life to the next. It is a lamp to our feet and, therefore, a light unto our path, even in the valley of the shadow (Ps 119:105).

With these certainties in mind, the words of David in Psalm 19 take on new meaning with respect to your path and his leading: "The law of the LORD is perfect, reviving the soul; the testimony of the LORD is sure, making wise the simple; the precepts of the LORD are right, rejoicing the heart; the commandment of the LORD is pure, enlightening the eyes; the fear of the LORD is clean, enduring forever; the rules of the LORD are true, and righteous altogether. More to be desired are they than gold, even much fine gold; sweeter also than honey and drippings of the honeycomb. Moreover, by them is your servant warned; in keeping them there is great reward. Who can discern his errors? Declare me innocent from hidden faults. Keep back your servant also from presumptuous sins; let them not have dominion over me! Then I shall be blameless, and innocent of great transgression. Let the words of my mouth and the meditation of my heart be acceptable in your sight, O LORD, my rock and my redeemer."

As these take on new meaning, so does the valley of the shadow of death. There is no fear but only comfort as our rock and redeemer leads us through it to our glorious home he has prepared.

May his word become a priority, a love, a passion, and a light for your way. May you find not just confidence and courage in it but comfort through the dark times of life.

Study Questions

(1) What are the guarantees we see in this section of Psalm 23?

(2) What does the image of "shadow" tell us and how does it help remove our fear of death?

(3) How do believers and non-believers view death differently? How does your view of death line up?

(4) How do you turn to God's word as a way to comfort you? Do you see it as a comfort? How do you value God's word?

(5) What scripture passages give you the most comfort and why?

(6) What does Psalm 19 say about how you should live? How does it impact how you view death?

Chapter 6
A Table in Eternity

"You prepare a table before me in the presence of my enemies; you anoint my head with oil; my cup overflows."
Psalm 23:5

Within the psalm, we have moved from life to death and back to life again. Because of the Good Shepherd and the fact that he laid down his life for his sheep, death no longer has a hold on us. In the movement of this psalm back to life, we see a picture of the great banquet of our Lord, we see our glory wrapped in his, and we see our inheritance. It is here that we celebrate the I Am of the Resurrection and the Life. Godfrey wrote: "The good news of Psalm 23 is that God accomplishes all this even in the presence of our enemies. Those who enjoy fellowship with Christ by faith will be revived and satisfied in this life, even in spite of the best efforts of our enemies. They may oppose us, but Christ the Good Shepherd will lead us, and His goodness and mercy will pursue us, until we arrive safely home."[1]

I shall not want... you prepare a table

This is a fulfillment of many passages in scripture as they look to the return of our Lord and Savior. Jesus, speaking to the people in Luke 14:15–24, says this: "When one of those who reclined at table with him heard these things, he said to him, 'Blessed is everyone who will eat bread in the kingdom of God!' But he said to him, 'A man once gave a great banquet and invited many. And at the time for the banquet he sent his servant to say to those who had been invited, 'Come, for everything is now ready.' But they all alike began to make excuses. The first said to him, 'I have bought a field, and I must go out and see it. Please have me excused.' And another said, 'I have bought five yoke of oxen, and I go to examine them. Please have me excused.' And another said, 'I have married a wife, and therefore I cannot come.' So the servant came and reported these things to his master. Then the master of the house became angry and said to his servant, 'Go out quickly to the streets and lanes of the city, and bring in the poor and crippled and blind and lame.' And the servant said, 'Sir, what you commanded has been done, and still there is room.' And the master said to the servant, 'Go out to the highways and hedges and compel people to come in, that my house may be filled. For I tell you, none of those men who were invited shall taste my banquet.'"

First, being invited to the great banquet was a blessing to those who could see and hear it. Why was being invited a blessing? You were in the presence of the one giving it; it was gracious to be invited; it was more than enough to satisfy. Do not miss this point: blessing is about being as close to the face of the King (God) as possible.

Second, the king demonstrates great patience as he invited many. How is the king patient? This was not a last-minute invitation. The invitation did not go out when he said the feast was ready. No, the invitation went out well before then. So, when the time came for the feast, he called out. One excuse after another, they rejected the king's invitation. At which point, he turned to others to invite them in. This is the fulfillment of the prophecy and covenant God made with Abraham. In Genesis 12:1-3, we are told that through Abraham the whole world would be blessed. Salvation was not just for the Jewish people, who were the direct descendants of Abraham, but would be offered to all the families of the earth. If you hear his voice calling today, do not turn away. The banquet he set before us, he invites you to attend.

Third, we see the king compelling those in the streets and on the highways to come to the banquet. How is this similar to the beginning of Psalm 23? Very similar in language to the beginning of this psalm: he makes, he leads, he restores. He has prepared a banquet and those whom he brings in, they will sit at the table.

Fourth, we see the banquet given in the presence of those who turned down the king. It was not that they left town. It was not that they somehow disappeared. They would have seen that the banquet still went on, just without them. We, too, come up with many excuses to not hear or come to the banquet. Will you turn away from the gospel invitation?

On that day, for those who are his, they will be brought to that table by the Good Shepherd. Just as before, he prepares a table. At the beginning of the Psalm, he made them lie down. He led them beside streams that were still. He restored their soul. He even carried them through the valley of the shadow. Now, he prepares a table. Nothing the sheep have done; everything the shepherd has done.

What will the banquet be like? This banquet will be a time of praise, joy, gladness, and rejoicing. As Isaiah 25:6-9 says: "On this mountain the LORD of hosts will make for all peoples a feast of rich food, a feast of well-aged wine, of rich food full of marrow, of aged wine well refined. And he will swallow up son this mountain the covering that is cast over all peoples, the veil that is spread over all nations. He will swallow up death forever; and the Lord GOD will wipe away tears from all faces, and the reproach of his people he will take away from all the earth, for the LORD has spoken. It will be said on that day, 'Behold, this is our God; we have waited for him, that he might save us. This is the LORD; we have waited for him; let us be glad and rejoice in his salvation.'"

And again, from Revelation 19:9: "And the angel said to me, 'Write this: Blessed are those who are invited to the marriage supper of the Lamb.'" This banquet is about blessing. Do not miss that, as it is amplified in the very next phrase.

I shall not want... you anoint my head with oil

We know that this banquet signifies blessing because of the phrase that follows: "...you anoint my head with oil." Godfrey says: "To be 'anointed with oil' here has the sense of enjoying the fragrant and refreshing oil that anoints our heads and makes our faces shine (Ps. 104:15; Luke 7:46). Those who sit at the Lord's table will be revived by His anointing oil."2

To see this beautifully illustrated, turn with me to Zechariah 3:1-5: "Then he showed me Joshua the high priest standing before the angel of the LORD, and Satan standing at his right hand to accuse him. And the LORD said to Satan, 'The LORD rebuke you, O Satan! The LORD who has chosen Jerusalem rebuke you! Is not this a brand plucked from the fire?' Now Joshua was standing before the angel, clothed with filthy garments. And the angel said to those who were standing before him, 'Remove the filthy garments from him' And to him he said, 'Behold, I have taken your iniquity away from you, and I will clothe you with pure vestments.' And I said, 'Let them put a clean turban on his head.' So they put a clean turban on his head and clothed him with garments. And the angel of the LORD was standing by."

So that you get the full thrust of this point, let your imagination go a little bit here in light of Luke 14:12-24. Joshua, the High Priest, had died. He stands before God. The banquet table was set. The enemies of Joshua gathered around. Satan makes accusations against Joshua, who has just been carried through the valley of the shadow of death. He was standing in judgment at what should have been a celebration. The King, seeing the invitation in hand, rebukes Satan. He takes the filthy garments from him and gives him new clothes, pure and holy. "I have plucked this one from the fire! Hands off." And to Joshua, God said: "Join the feast I have prepared for you." This picture is so beautiful and full of hope for a sinner such as I. Hear what Matthew Henry says: "He (God) parts between them and their sins, and so prevents their sins parting between them and their God; he reconciles himself to the sinner, but not to the sin."[3]

This section is about how God removes our guilt of sin and gives us righteousness, not our own, and how he makes peace with us in Christ (Rom. 4:4–5; 5:1). It is a picture of our justification by faith alone and our glorification. It is a picture of how his righteousness is imputed to us (Gal. 2:15–16; 2 Cor. 5:21). Zechariah 3 is the Old Testament version of Romans 8:33–34: "Who shall bring any charge against God's elect? It is God who justifies. Who is to condemn? Christ Jesus is the one who died—more than that, who was raised—who is at the right hand of God, who indeed is interceding for us."

This anointing is something he does for you. The

anointing at the Great Banquet sets us apart as ones who are forgiven and received, refreshed and renewed, and joyful and content. Sin kicked us out of the Garden of Eden in Genesis 3; God's anointing has restored to us once again Eden here at the table. As we look upon the banquet, we see him as enough. Revel in it; marvel in it; let it mark who you are, whom you belong to, and where you are going.

One last point before moving on. What is anointing? This anointing is a reviving of the spirit. Notice earlier in the Psalm the phrase: "He restores my soul." This points to our salvation found in him. The anointing points to the fact that we have been sanctified by the work of the Spirit and now come to the table having been glorified. When considering the ordo salutis (the order of salvation), we walk through the steps of salvation in the life of a believer: predestination, election, calling, regeneration, faith, repentance, justification, adoption, sanctification, perseverance, and glorification. We see that last step here in this verse. Throughout the previous two verses, we saw outlined the sanctification and perseverance. Now we have here illustrated the glorification (Romans 8:30, Psalm 49:15, Daniel 12:2, John 11:23–24, and 1 Corinthians 15:20).

I shall not want...my cup overflows

And now, we come to the end of this section where the psalmist, as he surveys his life, death, and resurrection, as he sees his inheritance in the King, as he rejoices sitting at the banquet table, he acknowledges again what he said at the beginning and even more than that. It is more than just: "I shall not want..." Now, the psalmist cries out: "My cup overflows..." The blessing of the King is even more than he imagined. The immensity of the greatness of his riches toward him, toward us, becomes obvious, and the psalmist cannot contain himself. This phrase points to what follows— dwelling with him forever. Hear the testimony from Scripture on this: "Let not your hearts be troubled. Believe in God; believe also in me. In my Father's house are many rooms. If it were not so, would I have told you that I go to prepare a place for you? And if I go and prepare a place for you, I will come again and will take you to myself, that where I am you may be also. And you know the way to where I am going" (John 14:1-3). "Blessed be the God and Father of our Lord Jesus Christ, who has blessed us in Christ with every spiritual blessing in the heavenly places...In him we have obtained an inheritance, having been predestined according to the purpose of him who works all things according to the counsel of his will, so that we who were the first to hope in Christ might be to the praise of his glory. In him you also, when you heard the word of truth, the gospel of your salvation, and believed in him, were sealed with the promised Holy Spirit, who is the guarantee of our inheritance until we acquire possession of it, to the praise of his glory" (Eph 1:3–14).

The Good Shepherd leads us faithfully to bring us home for his name sake. We sit at his table as did Mephibosheth at the table of David, wanting nothing under his care and glad in his king. From here, we point to the place Christ has gone to prepare for us in him. It is our promise, our inheritance, our hope. In that place, just as here and now, we find our Sabbath rest.

Study Questions

(1) Luke 14:15–24 – Why was being invited a blessing? Do you view your salvation as a blessing? How does it display itself in your life and relationships?

(2) Luke 14:15–24 – How was the king patient? How do you respond to his patience?

(3) What will the banquet be like? Isaiah 25:6–9

(4) What is anointing? How does God's anointing change you?

(5) What do you think about this? "And now, we come to the end of this section where the psalmist, as he surveys his life, death, and resurrection, as he sees his inheritance in the King, as he rejoices sitting at the banquet table, he acknowledges again what he said at the beginning and even more than that. It is more than just: 'I shall not want...' Now, the psalmist cries out: 'My cup overflows...' The blessing of the king is even more than he imagined."

Chapter 7

Goodness and Mercy

"Surely goodness and mercy shall follow me all the days of my life, and I shall dwell in the house of the LORD forever."
Psalm 23:6

As we see the certainties in the valley of the shadow, we find, at the end, great comforts. This last phrase of the Psalm contains several truths that, like the hounds of heaven, pursue with great efficacy. The way the verse starts out, it reminds us of the teaching of Jesus when he says: "Truly, truly I say unto you..." There is, at the start, a certainty given. "Surely..." the psalmist writes. In closing out the Psalm, the writer not only looks to what follows in the verse, but harkens back to everything said up to this point. It is something you can "take to the bank." And so, we start out by saying that in this life and the next, this thing is certain if you are his, he will hold you to the end. The New Testament equivalent to this would be the word "amen."

But it is not just in the word "surely" that we see this

certainty. In fact, the next 3 words emphasize this certainty when he says "goodness and mercy." Within these three words, we are introduced to the Shepherd's steadfast love. His goodness and mercy are given as a free gift, not coming from our good works lest we should boast. For those that are his, the promise is sure; they have the Shepherd's goodness and mercy. His steadfast love endures forever.

Where do we see the steadfast love of the Lord in this Psalm? We see it in the Good Shepherd's provision for the flock ("I shall not want"). We see it in how he gives us rest along the journey ("He makes me to lie down in pastures green"). We see it in how he finds for us places of safety that refresh ("He leads me beside waters still"). We see it in how he saves us and heals us ("He restores my soul"). We see it in how he providentially keeps us on the paths we should walk ("He leads me in paths of righteousness"). We see it in how he takes us through life, death, and into eternity ("Even though I walk through the valley of the shadow of death"). We see it in the inheritance he provides (He prepares a table...he anoints my head...gives me far more than I ever deserve). His steadfast love endures forever. His steadfast love covers our past, present, and future.

Scripture is full of stories to remind us of this. The great cloud of witnesses stands ready to cheer you on with their story of God's pursuit and keeping of them. We see this pictured in the life of Abraham as he gave Lot the choice of which land to settle in. We see this pictured in the life of Joseph as he refused to succumb to the temptation of Potiphar's wife. We see this pictured in Daniel as he risked everything to pray to God. We see this pictured in the fiery furnace prepared for Shadrach, Meshach, and Abednego as they refused to bend their knees to the gods of their day. We see this pictured as Peter is gently restored by our Lord on the beach after the resurrection. But this steadfast love is not just for them. It is for you. It is for me.

From here, we see the range to which goodness and mercy extend: "will follow me..." There is nothing we can do to lose it. We cannot outrun his goodness and mercy. We cannot hide from it. It follows us. The Lord pursued of us while we were yet sinners, while we were dead in our sins. There was nothing within us that would have prompted this. There was nothing good within us that would have made us something to be desired. Rather, it was about his mercy and goodness. This goodness and mercy, this steadfast love, hunts us when we are lost, claims us when we are in the pen, and drags us home when we don't know any other way. It does this while rejoicing in the found sheep.

In Luke 15:3–5, we see this pursuit in action: "So he {Jesus} told them this parable: 'What man of you, having a hundred sheep, if he has lost one of them, does not leave the ninety-nine in the open country, and go after the one that is lost, until he finds it? And when he has found it, he lays it on his shoulders, rejoicing." Again, we see this in the Parable of the Lost Coin. The Psalm shows us the duration of the goodness and mercy: "all the days of my life." We have already shown that those who are in Christ have life eternal. The Father's steadfast love covers your past, present, and future. The duration is for eternity and is pictured for us in Zechariah 3, as we saw previously.

He is the God of our past, present, and future. He is the God of Creation... He is the Good Shepherd of our Past. He is also the God of Salvation... He is the Good Shepherd of our Present. Finally, he is the God of Heaven... He is the Good Shepherd of our hope and future. Philippians 1 reminds us that the God who has carried us thus far will carry us to the end. We have a hope for the future.

Hebrews 12:25-29 talks about this promise and hope for the future. In talking about the things that can be shaken, the author points to things that cannot be shaken: God, his word, our relationship with him, and our future home with him. The author speaks about the "surety" of it throughout the chapter. The author speaks to the guarantee: "for our God is a consuming fire." He is the God of Heaven, our hope and future. Praise his name!

This leads us to the final phrase, where we are shown our ultimate place of happiness. "I shall dwell in the house of the Lord forever." Psalm 27:4 tells us: "One thing have I asked of the LORD, that will I seek after: that I may dwell in the house of the LORD all the days of my life, to gaze upon the beauty of the LORD and to inquire in his temple." Psalm 21:6 tells us: "For you make him most blessed forever; you make him glad with the joy of your presence."

What does this idea of "dwelling" look like? Why is it something to be desired? Jesus told his disciples he was leaving them to go prepare a place for them. This is the fulfillment of that promise. I can only imagine the renewal of my body and soul by the Good Shepherd. The emphasis not to miss here is "dwell in the house of the Lord forever."

It is in this place where perfect blessing is found, sin is no more, pain is no more, decay is no more, and rest can be found. This dwelling indicates the making of a home, a settling down, establishing a place in which to spend your days. It is similar to the Greek word used for the Spirit making a dwelling place in our hearts. The length of days in this phrase seems to be repeated over and over ("forever") to remind us of the very thing Moses and the prophets talked about for this day: that He will be our God and we will be His people. This forever is not just in the pursuit but in the dwelling as we find our place in His kingdom.

Study Questions

(1) Psalm 23:6 – What are some of the comforts mentioned in this verse?

(2) Where do we see the steadfast love of the Lord in this Psalm?

(3) What is repeated in Psalm 136? According to the Psalm 136, why should we worship and what has the LORD done for us? What has the Lord done for you?

(4) Write out your story in the format of Psalm 136.

(5) What does "dwelling" look like? Why is it something to be desired?

Chapter 8
A Workman Approved

"But as for you, continue in what you have learned and have firmly believed, knowing from whom you learned it and how from childhood you have been acquainted with the sacred writings, which are able to make you wise for salvation through faith in Christ Jesus." 2 Timothy 3:14-15

Jim Elliot and his friends had a passion for those who had never heard the gospel. In particular, they felt a call to reach the unreachable, the Auca Indian tribe in Ecuador. They trusted God for the provision of opening a door. On January 8, 1956, they were hopeful a door was opening to this people group. Little did Jim and the others realize it was the door to glory for them. As they went out to meet the approaching Aucas, 10 warriors came at them with their spears. Even though they were armed with guns and could defend themselves, they had made the decision not to fight back should this be the welcome. They were willing to die for the gospel rather than kill another who had not yet heard it. And so, they perished that day.[1] Elisabeth Elliot, his wife, wrote this summary about his life and death, which seems most appropriate to this passage:

"Jim's aim was to know God. His course, obedience – the only course that could lead to the fulfillment of his aim. His end was what some would call an extraordinary death, although in facing death he had quietly pointed out that many have died because of obedience to God. He and the other men with whom he died were hailed as heroes, 'martyrs.' I do not approve. Nor would they have approved. Is the distinction between living for Christ and dying for Him, after all, so great? Is not the second the logical conclusion of the first? Furthermore, to live for God is to die 'daily,' as the apostle Paul put it. It is to lose everything that we may gain Christ. It is in thus laying down our lives that we find them."[2]

So, what does this have to do with Psalm 23? At the beginning, I made the comment that the Psalm was typically something read at a funeral. I hope as we have walked through it, you have seen how much more benefit it would give to see it as a Psalm for life. If we are to live "so what" kind of lives, we need to understand this idea of being a workman approved. What Paul writes to Timothy is the same as what David writes in the Psalm: that if we are his and he is ours, then we must follow him where he goes and submit to the shepherd.

Paul, speaking about becoming a workman approved and the path of a workman approved, writes to Timothy about the loves of the heart and how, by seeing the affections of a person's life, you can tell who owns their heart. Are they a workman approved or one deceived by the loves of the lures of this world? What did Jesus mean, after all, when he said: "Follow me?"

David Platt wrote these words in his book *Radical*: "You and I desperately need to consider whether we have ever truly, authentically trusted in Christ for our salvation. In this light Jesus' words at the end of the Sermon on the Mount are some of the most humbling in all of Scripture. 'Not everyone who says to me, 'Lord, Lord,' will enter the kingdom of heaven, but only he who does the will of my Father who is in heaven. Many will say to me on that day, 'Lord, Lord, did we not prophesy in your name, and in your name drive out demons and perform many miracles?' Then I will tell them plainly, 'I never knew you. Away from me, you evildoers!' Jesus was not speaking here to irreligious people, atheists, or agnostics. He was not speaking to pagans or heretics. He was speaking to devoutly religious people who were deluded into thinking they were on the narrow road that leads to heaven when they were actually on the broad road that leads to hell. According to Jesus, one day not just a few but many will be shocked — eternally shocked — to find that they were not in the kingdom of God after all."[3]

And so, at the end of this journey we have taken through Psalm 23, I ask you this question: "Where are your affections today?" How you answer this question drives the path that is taken in life. Know this, the path of a workman approved is driven by, is rooted in, and finds its beginning and end in Christ and what he has done for you. This is critical to understand. You cannot manufacture the path of a workman approved. You can try. You might even deceive those in the church and yourself that you are on the path of the workman approved. That is why it is so important that you get this right.

In this chapter, we will look at misplaced affections, what characterizes the path of a workman approved, and how you become a workman approved.

First, Paul begins this section of his letter to Timothy

talking about misplaced affections with this phrase: "But understand this..." This is more than just an instruction for what is to follow but very much a link to what he just finished saying. In 2 Timothy 2, Paul encourages Timothy to: "Do your best to present yourself to God as one approved, a worker who has no need to be ashamed, rightly handling the word of truth." He wants Timothy to not lose heart, be deceived, or become sidetracked and thus shipwreck his faith. He wants Timothy to know that even as he seeks the peace and purity of the Church through the Gospel, there will be those who do not. And so he warns him that "in the last days there will be times of difficulty."

Now, to be clear, the phrase "in the last days" is frequently misunderstood in our day. Paul was not talking about some time in the distance that Timothy would not see. When scripture refers to the last days, it simply talks about the time between Christ's first and second coming. To be clear, it points to the whole time between the first and second coming, not just the period right before his return. So, from our vantage point, what Paul wants Timothy to understand, he wants us to understand as well. For in our time, just as in his and just as in the time to come, there will be times of difficulty. There will be weeds that grow within the harvest. There will be wheat with the chaff. There will be wolves in the midst of the sheep. We must understand this and be on the lookout. We must rightly handle the word of truth and present ourselves to God as one approved and unashamed.

It is important to note that Paul is not talking about those outside the church. One would think, reading through this list, that Paul was taking direct aim at the world. He wasn't. We are to be on the lookout for those within the church who are "lovers of self," "lovers of money," and "lovers of pleasure." These are the loves of this world. These were at the heart of the temptation. They are antithetical to the love of God and the love of others and are contrary to the gospel. James Boice wrote: "To love the world is to increasingly drift from love for God and thereby also lose love for others."

Jesus referred to the loves of this world as the world, the flesh, and the devil in the Parable of the Sower. John put it this way: "Do not love the world or the things in the world. If anyone loves the world, the love of the Father is not in him. For all that is in the world—the desires of the flesh and the desires of the eyes and pride of life—is not from the Father but is from the world. And the world is passing away along with its desires, but whoever does the will of God abides forever." Those who place such a high value on these loves find themselves, as this passage states, being: "proud, arrogant, abusive, disobedient to their parents, ungrateful, unholy, heartless, unappeasable, slanderous, without self-control, brutal, not loving good, treacherous, reckless, swollen with conceit...having the appearance of godliness, but denying its power."

We see in our time, as in the past, the lure of the loves of this world. From the accumulation of stuff to coveting to our own boasting to complaining and thus showing a complete lack of grace.

Paul contrasts the love of this world with the love of God. To be a lover of this world is to not be a lover of God. Perhaps we ought to hear this again: to be a lover of this world is not to be a lover of God. Understand this, you cannot serve two masters. The love of this world does not share a bed with the love of God. The lack of contentment doesn't coexist with the rest found in the Sabbath of our Lord. The pursuit of things leading to destruction doesn't find its end in things eternal. You cannot hold the hand of Satan and the hand of the Lord. You must make a choice. So, Paul, in his warning to the church, is asking the question, "Where are your affections?" What is it that you seek after? What is it that holds your attention? What is it that you truly treasure?

Jesus, on the road to Caesarea Philippi, asked his disciples this question, a question that transcends time and place, "Who do men say that I the Son of Man am?" Who do you say that he is? Is he just a good teacher? A prophet? Or is he the Son of the Living God? Is your Christ too small? What value do you place upon Christ? Do you love him with all of who you are? Or do you follow after the lures of this world? Where are your affections today?

So, what characterizes the path of a workman approved? First, a workman approved listens to his word. This comes from reading scripture, meditating upon it, and obeying his word. Paul said this to Timothy: "But as for you, continue in what you have learned and have firmly believed, knowing from whom you learned it and how from childhood you have been acquainted with the sacred writings, which are able to make you wise for salvation through faith in Christ Jesus."

Scripture tells us:

- "Man shall not live by bread alone but by every word that proceeds from the mouth of God."

- "Thy word, Oh Lord, is a light unto my feet and a lamp unto my path."

- "How can a young man keep his way pure? By guarding it according to your word. With my whole heart I seek you; let me not wander from your commandments! I have stored up your word in my heart that I might not sin against you..."

- "In the way of your testimonies, I delight as much as in all riches. I will meditate on your precepts and fix my eyes on your ways. I will delight in your statutes; I will not forget your word."

Indeed, the path of a workman approved starts with listening to his word. This isn't just a casual opening of his word. But, as Paul indicates here, how from childhood Timothy was "acquainted with the sacred writings." His life was built upon the word of God. Paul doesn't stop there, though. Just because Timothy had been well acquainted with scripture since his youth, it was no reason to stop or set aside the treasuring of God's word. Paul commands Timothy to "continue in what you have learned and firmly believed..."

The same is true for us. Do we treasure God's word as a guiding lamp unto our feet? Do we store up his word in our hearts that we might not sin against him? Do we delight in his word? All of his word? Is it something we meditate upon? The path of a workman approved begins in the word of God. A workman approved is well acquainted with scripture and continues to study it. R. C. Sproul, while commenting on this passage in his book *Knowing Scripture*, writes: "The Christian who is not diligently involved in a serious study of Scripture is simply inadequate as a disciple of Christ. To be an adequate Christian and competent in the things of God one must do more than attend 'sharing sessions' and 'bless-me parties.' We cannot learn competency by osmosis. The biblically illiterate Christian is not only inadequate but unequipped."[4]

Second, a workman approved understands that obedience is a transformed life, not a list of do's and don'ts observed. Paul put it this way in our passage: "All Scripture is breathed out by God and profitable for teaching, for reproof, for correction, and for training in righteousness, that the man of God may be complete, equipped for every good work." Salvation leads to a restored relationship with God and a new life. It is through teaching, reproof, correction, and training in righteousness that we see transformation. Notice, he calls scripture profitable. The life he leads you to is advantageous to you, profitable, good. It is not a list of do's and don'ts. Rather, it is a lifestyle that stems from a changed heart.

This is what we see in 1 Corinthians 13, the great chapter on love. If you read through that chapter, you will see how love is described, not as a list of adjectives but as verbs and actions. It is not a one-time event but a way of life. It is driven by what Christ has done on our behalf.

That is what we see in Exodus 20. The whole of the 10 Commandments was never intended to be a checklist. Rather, it was designed for us, in response to what God has done for us, to ask the questions like:

- If I am not to murder, then what should I do? How do I support life? Whose life do I value? Do I keep the gospel to myself, helping to send a soul to eternal death? Or...

- If I am not to steal, then what should I do? Do I hold on too tightly to the things of this world? Do I fail to give to God what is his? When I see my neighbor in need and I have what they need, do I turn away or gladly open my hand? Am I uncomfortable amidst the poor and needy? Or do I welcome them with open arms?

The 10 Commandments are not a list of do's and don'ts. Rather, they are a clear picture of what Paul describes as love in 1 Corinthians 13. It is the picture of a transformed life.

Third, a workman approved learns and works in the community. Paul writes: "But as for you, continue in what you have learned and have firmly believed, knowing from whom you learned it..." There is a clear picture of not living and learning and working alone in the work God has for his people. At the start of the letter, he says: "I am reminded of your sincere faith, which first lived in your grandmother Lois and in your mother Eunice and, I am persuaded, now lives in you also." And, again: "Rather, join with me in suffering for the gospel, by the power of God. He has saved us and called us to a holy life—not because of anything we have done but because of his own purpose and grace." The writer of Hebrews exhorts his readers not to abandon the regular gathering of believers. Scripture is full of "one another" statements that point to life in the faith being life in a community. Indeed, a workman approved learns and works in community.

Fourth, a workman approved has work to do. Paul wrote to Timothy: "All Scripture is breathed out by God and profitable for teaching, for reproof, for correction, and for training in righteousness, that the man of God may be complete, equipped for every good work." In his letter to the Ephesians, Paul writes this: "For by grace you have been saved through faith. And this is not your own doing; it is the gift of God, not a result of works, so that no one may boast. For we are his workmanship, created in Christ Jesus for good works, which God prepared beforehand, that we should walk in them."

David Platt writes in his book *Radical*: "One of the unintended consequences of contemporary church strategies that revolve around performances, places, programs, and professionals is that somewhere along the way people get left out of the picture. But according to Jesus, people are God's method for winning the world to himself. People who have been radically transformed by Jesus. People who are not sidelined to sit in a chair on Sundays while they watch professionals take care of ministry for them. People who are equipped on Sundays to participate in ministry every day of the week. People who are fit and free to do precisely what Jesus did and what Jesus told us to do. Make disciples...Jesus beckons each of us to plainly, humbly, and quietly focus our lives on people."[5]

Is your affection misplaced? What must you do to become a workman approved? Christ alone makes you a workman approved. Being a workman approved has nothing to do with you, what you do, or what you have done. It has everything to do with the person and work of Christ. It has everything to do with what Jesus did for you. Paul says to Timothy in this passage: "But as for you, continue in what you have learned and have firmly believed, knowing from whom you learned it and how from childhood you have been acquainted with the sacred writings, which are able to make you wise for salvation through faith in Christ Jesus." Paul put it this way in his letter to the Romans that the gospel is the power of God for the salvation of everyone who believes (Rom 1:16). Solomon wrote that the fear of the Lord is the beginning of wisdom (Prov 1:7). James said in his letter that if anyone lacks wisdom, he should ask God who gives generously to all without finding fault and that it would be given to him. But James reminds us, when he asks, he must believe and not doubt (James 1:5-6). Dear reader, it is "by grace you have been saved through faith. And this is not your own doing; it is the gift of God, not a result of works, so that no one may boast. For we are his workmanship, created in Christ Jesus for good works, which God prepared beforehand, that we should walk in them" (Eph 2:8-10).

A true faith is a living faith. Salvation is not about some prayer prayed or an aisle walked. It is about faith alone in Christ alone, according to scripture alone, to the glory of God alone. Being a workman approved is about a rightly placed affection granted by the king.

That being said, what is it that we believe? It is simple. First, Christ came to live the perfect life that we couldn't. Second, Christ paid the penalty for sin that we deserved; he paid it in full. Third, Christ rose from the grave, conquering sin and death, ensuring our eternal life with him.

Who or what do you believe in? If Christ does not hold the only place, repent and call upon Christ as Lord and Savior. Believe that he was indeed raised from the dead. Begin to live with that in mind.

There was a famine in the land. This was not just a physical famine but a spiritual famine as well. For 3 years, rain did not fall on the land. At the end of 3 years, a challenge was issued. The man of God called upon the king of the land to a showdown on Mount Carmel. The people gathered to watch, one man against hundreds. Elijah was that man. As he drew near to the people, he said: "How long will you go limping between two different opinions? If the LORD is God, follow him; but if Baal, then follow him" (1 Kings 18:21). The people did not answer him; they remained quiet.

If we are to live "so what" kind of lives, we cannot remain silent. We need to, by grace through faith, call upon the name of the Lord for salvation. We need to see that we are his and he is ours. Because the gospel changes everything, we need to follow him where he goes and submit to the shepherd. Our faith needs to be alive, walking and talking and working and playing.

Will you remain quiet this day? Dear reader, how long will you waver between two positions? If God is God, then serve him. Turn to Jesus, and you will find rest. Turn to him, and you will find grace and forgiveness. Turn to him, and you will find purpose and hope. There will be difficulty, yes. But he has overcome and in that you can rest. Cling to the gospel for it is "able to make you wise for salvation through faith in Christ Jesus."

Study Questions

(1) If you opened up your checkbook or looked at your credit card statement or made a detailed account of how you spent each day, where would you say your affections lay?

(2) If you walked through the 10 commandments with the thought process — "If I am not supposed to do this, then what should I do," does that change anything for you?

(3) When you are looking for a church, where do "programs" rank?

(4) What do you think about this: "A true faith is a living faith. Salvation is not about some prayer prayed or an aisle walked. It is about faith alone in Christ alone according to scripture alone to the glory of God alone. Being a workman approved is about a rightly placed affection granted by the king."

(5) Is your affection misplaced? What must you do to become a workman approved?

Notes

All Scripture references are from the ESV except where noted.

Chapter 1: I Am His and He Is Mine

1. John Piper, "Maintain the Unity of the Spirit," Desiring God, https://www.desiringgod.org/messages/maintain-the-unity-of-the-spirit

2. Matthew Henry, *Matthew Henry's Commentary* (New York: Revell Company, 1935) 5:490

Chapter 2: His Provision, Providence, and Protection

1. Michael G. McKelvey, "He makes me lie down in green pastures. He leads me beside still waters." *Tabletalk*, August 2018, 11

2. "Matthew Henry's Commentary on Psalms", Bible Study Tools, https://www.biblestudytools.com/commentaries/matthew-henry-complete/psalms/23.html

3. "Matthew Henry's Commentary on Psalms", Bible Study

Tools,

https://www.biblestudytools.com/commentaries/matthew-henry-complete/psalms/23.html

Chapter 3: For His Name Sake

1. J I Packer, *Concise Theology* (Illinois:Tyndale House Publishers, 1993), 241

2. "Spurgeon's Verse Expositions on John," Studylight.org, https://www.studylight.org/commentaries/eng/spe/john-17.html

3. "Be still my soul: the Lord is on thy side by Kathrina von Schlegel", Hymnary.org,

https://hymnary.org/text/be_still_my_soul_the_lord_is_on_thy_side

Chapter 4: His Love Endures Forever

1. Dr. Goldsmith, *An Abridgement of the History of England* (London: H. Mozley, Gainsborough, 1807), 22–23

2. Dr Charles Stanley, "Things that Cannot Be Shaken," InTouch.org,

https://www.intouch.org/watch/sermons/things-that-cannot-be-shaken

Chapter 5: The Valley of the Shadow

1. Charles Spurgeon, *O Death, Where is Your Sting* (Illinois: Cross-Points Books, 2021), 6

2. Charles Spurgeon, *O Death, Where is Your Sting* (Illinois: Cross-Points Books, 2021), 76

3. Charles Spurgeon, *O Death, Where is Your Sting* (Illinois: Cross-Points Books, 2021), 12

4. Charles Spurgeon, *O Death, Where is Your Sting* (Illinois: Cross-Points Books, 2021), 27

5. Charles Spurgeon, *O Death, Where is Your Sting* (Illinois: Cross-Points Books, 2021), 27

6. Charles Spurgeon, *O Death, Where is Your Sting* (Illinois: Cross-Points Books, 2021), 101

7. Charles Spurgeon, *O Death, Where is Your Sting* (Illinois: Cross-Points Books, 2021), 101

8. Charles Spurgeon, *Miracles and Parables of Our Lord* (Michigan: Baker Book House, 2003), 1:353

9. Charles Spurgeon, *O Death, Where is Your Sting* (Illinois:

Cross-Points Books, 2021), 39-40

10. Charles Spurgeon, *O Death, Where is Your Sting* (Illinois: Cross-Points Books, 2021), 10

11. Charles Spurgeon, *O Death, Where is Your Sting* (Illinois: Cross-Points Books, 2021), 9-10

Chapter 6: A Table in Eternity

1. William Godfrey, "An Uncomfortable Table," Ligonier, August 7,2021,

https://www.ligonier.org/learn/devotionals/an-uncomfortable-table

2. William Godfrey, "An Uncomfortable Table," Ligonier, August 7,2021,

https://www.ligonier.org/learn/devotionals/an-uncomfortable-table

3. "Matthew Henry's Commentary on Zechariah", Bible Study Tools,

https://www.biblestudytools.com/commentaries/matthew-henry-complete/zechariah/3.html

Chapter 8: A Workman Approved

1. "Jim Elliot: Story and Legacy," ChristianityToday.com, https://www.christianity.com/church/church-history/timeline/1901-2000/jim-elliot-no-fool-11634862.html

2. Elisabeth Elliot, *Shadow of the Almighty* (New York:Haper One, 1989), 9-10

3. David Platt, Radical (Colorado: Multnomah Books, 2010), 37-38

4. RC Sproul, *Knowing Scripture* (Illinois: InterVarsity Press, 1977), 23

5. David Platt, Radical (Colorado: Multnomah Books, 2010), 90-91

About the Author

Daniel Rogers has served as an elder in his denomination since 2006. His ministry has included leading mission trips both internationally and domestically, youth and college groups, community groups, Sunday school classes, communicant classes, and church missions. Rogers has taught extensively to congregations across the country. He lives in the Elgin, Illinois, area with his wife, Jane, and their puppy. They have three children and three grandchildren.

www.ingramcontent.com/pod-product-compliance
Lightning Source LLC
Chambersburg PA
CBHW071800120626
46550CB00002B/862